HER Legacy

A Tribute to Elaine LaLanne's Impact on Health, Wellness and Empowerment.

By **Elaine LaLanne**

And 14 Authors Carrying Her Legacy Forward

With Introductions by Cathe Friedrich, Amy Boone Thompson and Lynn Allison

ISBN: 979-8-9854421-1-3

Scriptor
PUBLISHING GROUP

ScriptorPublishingGroup.com

Table of Contents

Part 1: Elaine's Story

Part 2: Her Legacy

Part 3: LaLa-isms

Editor's Note

Following Elaine "LaLa" LaLanne's introduction, you'll notice something unique about this book. *HER Legacy* is not just a memoir, and it's not just a tribute. It's a collaborative project – a gathering of voices, stories, and lessons from people whose lives and work have been touched by LaLa.

Elaine begins the book in Part I by sharing her own story including her partnership with Jack, her philosophies on vitality, and her role as the "keeper of the flame." But LaLa's legacy doesn't live in one person's story alone. It lives in the ripples she created through the family members she loved, the fitness icons she inspired, the friends she uplifted, and the generations of leaders who followed her example.

That's why Part II of this book opens the stage to a few co-authors, each offering a chapter of their own. You'll read how LaLa's influence shaped their journeys, and how they, in turn, are carrying her spirit of strength, generosity, and joy into the world.

Part III closes with timeless lessons – what we like to call "La-La-isms" – which are practical ways to live with vitality at any age, so you, too, can carry her message forward.

Our hope is that as you read these stories, you'll not only discover the remarkable life of Elaine LaLanne but also see your own reflection in these pages. Because *HER Legacy* isn't just Elaine's story. It's an invitation for all of us to consider the legacy we are building with our own lives.

A Tribute To Elaine LaLanne

By Cathe Friedrich

Founder of Cathe Friedrich Fitness and
2011 Inductee into the National Fitness Hall of Fame

A legacy is not only built but is woven into the world. Elaine LaLanne is more than just a living legacy. She exemplifies what it means to weave your uniqueness, your kindness, and your message into everyone and everything that you touch. Long before health and fitness became a global movement, Elaine stood passionately by the side of her husband, the legendary Jack LaLanne. While Jack often took center stage as the face and voice of a growing movement, Elaine was undeniably the heart, devotedly standing behind a message that she truly believed in. With determination, strength, and poise, she continues to spread this message and empowers the world with every heartbeat.

A trailblazer in her own right, Elaine lives the life that she so authentically preaches. A life that prioritizes health and wellness, that revels in the ability to be of service to others, and that embraces the beauty of aging with purpose and passion. At the age of 99, she radiates energy and enthusiasm, reminding us that it's never too late to embrace movement, offer kindness, recognize your potential, and to lead bravely with your heart.

This book, *HER Legacy*, sprung from that very spirit. It's more than a beautiful tribute to Elaine; it embodies the powerful ripple effect that she has inspired. These pages hold the personal stories of 14 extraordinary women who, like Elaine, chose a path dedicated to health, service, and empowerment. But they aren't just stories. Each one is a journey as unique as the woman who lived it. Immerse yourself in their words as they share these journeys, where conquering challenges, embracing resilience, and finding their own strength, has helped them to transform lives.

The title, *HER Legacy*, was chosen not only to honor Elaine and her influence on the world of health and fitness, but also to highlight a movement that Elaine helped to ignite and continues to fuel. A movement that encourages women to step forward with courage, give selflessly, lead boldly with passion, and to stay true to their individuality. With resilience and unwavering determination, Elaine continues to live her message and indomitably inspires all women to do the same.

To the leaders, the learners, the listeners. To the fitness professionals, wellness enthusiasts, and those who are still working on bettering their health. To those seeking encouragement, strength, or fresh inspiration. This book is for you. We will all discover a piece of ourselves in these stories. True strength is more than muscle- it's about spirit, heart, and being part of something greater than yourself. Let the words on these pages ignite a new fire within in you, while honoring the woman who helped to start it all.

This is HER Legacy. And now, it will be woven into yours.

Presence Over Perfection
A Tribute to Elaine LaLanne's Living Legacy

By Amy Boone Thompson

Owner & CEO, IDEA® Health & Fitness Association, IDEA World®

When I received the invitation to introduce **HER Legacy** in honor of Elaine LaLanne's 100th birthday, I was both honored and deeply humbled. To write about a woman whose life has been a masterclass in purposeful living is a privilege – and a responsibility I do not take lightly. Elaine – known affectionately to so many as "LaLa" and the "**First Lady of Fitness**" – has shaped our profession and inspired generations. Her journey is not merely a testament to longevity; it is a vibrant, ongoing love letter to discipline, joy, and service – a narrative that challenges us all to redefine what it means to leave a mark on this world.

In an era obsessed with speed, perfection, and fleeting recognition, Elaine LaLanne stands as a beacon of enduring presence and meaningful action. Her life is a reminder that legacy is not a destination, but a daily practice – a mosaic crafted through moments of generosity, consistency, and authentic connection. Elaine's story matters now more than ever because she embodies the kind of discipline that is rooted not in rigidity, but in joy and a deep sense of purpose. Her discipline is not about self-denial; it is about self-respect, about honoring the vessel that allows us to serve, to love, and to contribute.

There is a subtle but profound difference between success and significance. Success is often measured by external milestones – accolades, achievements, applause. Significance, however, is measured by the depth of our impact, the lives we touch, and the wisdom we pass on. Elaine LaLanne is the rare individual who has achieved both. Her legacy is not built on perfection, but on presence – on showing up, day after day, with grace and generosity. Through her work, her mentorship, and her unwavering commitment to health and hope, Elaine has shown that significance is born from a life lived in service to others.

Elaine's life is a living invitation to "pass it on" – to make health, hope, and helping others a daily practice. She reminds us that legacy is not a grand gesture, but a series of small, intentional acts. It is in the encouragement we offer, the wisdom we share, and the kindness we extend. Elaine's example teaches us that anyone can be a torchbearer, lighting the way for others through presence and consistency.

My personal connection to LaLa began through **IDEA® Health & Fitness Association**, where since 2011, we have presented the IDEA® Jack LaLanne Award at our annual **IDEA® World Convention**. This award was created to honor both Jack, recognizing those who have consistently used their media platform to inspire millions to move more. In 2024, we made the decision to officially add Elaine's name, renaming this lifetime achievement to the "**IDEA® Jack & Elaine LaLanne Award**" – a gesture of deep respect for her own legacy, independent of Jack's and in recognition of her continued impact since his passing. That same year, Elaine was also the recipient of the **2024 IDEA® Fitness Inspiration Award,** a testament to the indelible mark she has made on our community and beyond.

As owner of IDEA, I have had the privilege of working with LaLa on five major events. I have visited her home and spent meaningful time with her children. These experiences have given me a first-hand view of her warmth, generosity, and authenticity. LaLa is truly one of the kindest, most considerate, and loving people I have ever met. Her ability to make everyone feel valued and seen is not just a trait – it is her legacy in action. Whether she is onstage inspiring thousands or sharing a quiet conversation in her living room, her presence is a gift.

In my own journey, I have learned that leadership is not about possessing all the answers, but about asking the right questions and being present for others. Elaine's legacy is a powerful reminder that our greatest influence comes not from what we achieve, but from how we make others feel – valued, seen, and inspired to become their best selves.

As you turn the pages of **HER Legacy**, I invite you to lean in – to listen not just to Elaine's words, but to the heartbeat of her life. Let her example challenge you to consider your own life's work – not as a distant aspiration, but as a living, breathing practice. Embrace the power of presence, the discipline of consistency, and the joy of service. Allow Elaine's story to inspire you to "pass it on", each and every day.

This is not just Elaine's legacy – it is an invitation to all of us, a call to live with greater purpose, generosity, and grace. May we honor her example by choosing significance over success, presence over perfection, and service above all.

A Tribute to Elaine's Legacy

By Lynn Allison

Reporter for Newsmax

When I heard that Elaine "LaLa" LaLanne was writing yet another book at the age of 99, I was obviously impressed. Sure, she is one of the brightest, most positive people on this planet but, as a writer, I know just how much time and energy it takes to put a book together, especially one filled with decades of memories.

So, when I was asked to write an introduction to HER Legacy, I was stumped. Where do I begin paying tribute to my icon? Well, let's start by saying in the nearly 50 years I've known Elaine, I've yet to hear her utter a negative or unkind word. Yes, she's a tough lady and disciplined in the typical LaLanne manner, but her kindness and compassion for everyone simply shines through.

And she's brilliant. We've had many conversations over the years during which she was able to recall people, places and events in the past with such detail and accuracy, I was completely blown away. Her mind and memory are sharper than most of us who are years younger.

I'm glad that the new book is about HER legacy. It's Elaine's words and her legend that we are finally celebrating. So many of her books have been written with her late husband, the legendary Jack LaLanne, and focused on his LaLanne-isms. And of course, the last best-seller,

Pride & Discipline, was written along with Greg Justice, sharing stories and anecdotes from and about the many famous people Jack touched during his illustrious lifetime.

Now it's HER turn. As she says in the new book, she and Jack were a team. There was no follow-the-leader. Elaine is a smart businesswoman, and she was instrumental in steering the LaLanne legacy with her wit, beauty and intelligence.

Even as she approaches her 100th birthday, Elaine continues to push the envelope. She still performs her morning jackknife exercises and her kitchen counter pushups. She takes care of business, continuing to write and do her podcasts on healthy living and aging. This kind of work ethic is so rare these days, but she's never judgmental about what others do with their lives. I can recall many times when I'd ask for quote or two about her philosophy or advice and within minutes, I'd receive a reply even when it was very early morning in California.

And that lovely sense of humor never ceases to inspire me. I look forward to our phone calls knowing I'll not only learn something from Elaine but get off the phone with a sense of joy having spent time with her. She told television celebrity Rachael Ray once on air that one secret she and Jack shared was the ability to laugh at their problems.

For example, one day she told me that she had fallen flat on her face as she went to get ice cream from the kitchen. She had stitches on her nose and jokingly said that her doctor took out the stitches at dinner one evening when he invited her to his home. She made the horrific experience light-hearted.

Another time she joked that people often asked her if she married Jack for his body. "I really didn't," she quips. "I married him for his mind and kind heart."

Sure, she's had medical challenges this decade, but Elaine simply accepts them and laughs. "It's what you get when you get older," she says. "It's part of life."

And what a friend! Both Jack and Elaine never failed to send me their annual holiday newsletter. When I was working for Globe magazine and a reporter would contact Jack for a story or quote, he'd always ask how I was. In times of trouble, Elaine always had the right advice: "Make a decision and take action!"

In her new book, I was surprised to learn that Elaine was painfully shy as a young girl. The fact that writing gave her an outlet should be of no surprise because it's the tool many of us use to overcome shyness. Writing helps us share our feelings when the spoken word may be intimidating. Certainly, in reading her books, you know that Elaine speaks to us from the heart. She wants everyone to be healthy and happy and really, that's what keeps her motivated. She obviously overcame her shyness and has spoken before thousands at the annual IDEA convention and other venues, and of course, on television.

One of her most adoring admirers is the talented actor Mark Wahlberg who is slated to play Jack LaLanne in an upcoming film. The look of love he gives her as she works out alongside him, says it all: This is a woman who is admired and respected by everyone she meets.

Elaine is most certainly human and not a Pollyanna. I called her one day just after she put her dog to sleep. It was the only time I had ever heard her sad, and we talked about it philosophically. But she doesn't dwell on the negative and soon had only positive memories to talk about when she spoke of Tootles. Jack had little patience for negative thinking and Elaine shares this philosophy.

I've learned just by being in her presence, either on the phone or online, that this is a woman with her own power, her own force of nature.

After Jack passed, she carried on and is still spreading the word of positive thinking, positive actions, and a positive lifestyle. HER Legacy will live on thanks to the incredible energy she exudes and shares. As a woman, I am in awe and admiration of how she lives her life and what she has contributed to ours. As a friend, I am blessed to know her, and I hope everyone who reads this book will also be inspired.

Read it, share it with your daughters, and know there is much strength in quiet wisdom paired with honesty, humor and dedication.

Foreword

By Greg Justice

Owner, AYC Health & Fitness, 2017 National Fitness Hall of Fame Inductee, Competitor on NBCs American Ninja Warrior

There are some people who build a life. There are others who build a legacy. Elaine LaLanne has done both.

I have spent decades in the fitness profession. I have trained thousands of clients. I have studied the science, respected the pioneers, and worked alongside leaders who shaped our industry. Very few individuals embody what this profession was meant to represent in the way Elaine does.

Strength. Service. Joy.

Her influence extends far beyond a stage, a studio, or a television screen. It lives in the example she sets each day.

This book is not a look backward. It is a living reflection of impact that continues to unfold.

Elaine's life has always been anchored in action. She did not stand behind the movement that Jack LaLanne started. She stood beside it. She carried it forward. She strengthened it. She protected it. When the spotlight faded, she continued to show up. That consistency is what defines her.

In a world that often celebrates visibility, Elaine represents something deeper. She represents commitment. The kind that shows up in private. The kind that endures when applause fades. The kind that chooses purpose again tomorrow.

I have watched her encourage others long after the cameras stopped rolling. I have seen her choose gratitude in moments that would have discouraged most people. I have witnessed a woman who understands that leadership begins with personal responsibility.

The fitness industry has changed over the years. Trends come and go. Equipment evolves. Marketing shifts. What does not change is the need for character. The need for integrity. The need for leaders who practice what they promote.

Elaine lives what she teaches.

Her message has never been complicated. Take care of your body. Honor your word. Serve others. Protect your independence. Those principles sound simple, yet they require discipline. And discipline is a form of self-respect.

This book gathers voices from individuals who have felt her influence personally. Each contributor brings a unique perspective. Each story carries a thread of gratitude. Together, they form a tapestry that reflects the reach of one life lived with intention.

As you read these pages, you will notice something consistent. The authors are not writing about a celebrity. They are writing about a mentor. A friend. A woman who made them feel seen. That is the true measure of impact.

Elaine's legacy is not defined by longevity alone. It is defined by relevance. She continues to speak into conversations that matter. She continues to inspire younger generations to value strength and purpose.

She continues to remind us that aging is not a decline. It is an opportunity to model what is possible.

I often say that independence is the real flex. Elaine embodies that idea. Her commitment to movement, to discipline, to optimism has preserved more than physical vitality. It has preserved freedom. Freedom to live fully. Freedom to serve. Freedom to lead by example.

There is a humility in her strength that is rare. She does not seek recognition. She seeks contribution. That posture has shaped countless lives.

For me personally, Elaine represents continuity. She connects the founding spirit of our industry to its future. She reminds us that the mission was never about aesthetics. It was about vitality. It was about helping people stay capable. It was about protecting dignity through movement.

This book carries that mission forward.

As you turn each page, I encourage you to read with reflection. Consider how one person's steady commitment can influence families, communities, and professions. Consider how daily discipline shapes decades. Consider what legacy means in your own life.

Legacy is not an event. It is a pattern of choices repeated over time.

Elaine LaLanne chose strength. She chose service. She chose to stand firm in her values. Because of that, others stand taller.

It has been my honor to know her. It is my privilege to contribute these words. And it is my hope that every reader walks away inspired to protect their health, honor their purpose, and build something that lasts.

Elaine has shown us that vitality has no expiration date.

Now it is our turn to carry it forward.

IDEA - Elaine, Jack and Greg

PART 1:

Elaine's Story

Not Just One Woman's Story

By Elaine "LaLa" LaLanne

Greg Justice asked me to write about my life and my Legacy for my 100th birthday in a book called *HER Legacy.*

I answered by saying, "I don't have a legacy! That's for people who are famous - like presidents, inventors or movie stars."

Having a legacy never entered my mind. In talking with him, he convinced me that everyone has a legacy. He told me he had many other contributors, but he wanted the first chapters to include stories about my life, how I evolved, and what I've learned through a century.

It started with a ripple on the water that continued to grow one after the other for the last 100 years. Therefore, I offer you my philosophy and snippets of my life that makes me "tick." In other words, what I think is my legacy.

So welcome to my life and my story about how I became involved with Jack LaLanne and the fitness industry.

Chapter 1

My Roots – And Seeds of My Legacy

Small Victories, Big Lessons

"You learned to swim, didn't you?"

Those words from my father still echo in my ears. He believed in perseverance and self-reliance. He believed in facing the things that scared you and coming out stronger. And he always gave me both sides of every story.

When he asked that question, I didn't realize that it was a seed that gave me confidence in myself and probably the way I lived my life and the meaning of perseverance.

I was born in Minnesota, the land of 10,000 lakes and grew up in Minneapolis which had 13. When I graduated from the 6th grade our principal gave the class a little booklet called "Keys to Success." As I recall it had some of the same core values of life that are given to the young golfers of the First Tee youth golf organization today. Values such as honesty, integrity, responsibility, perseverance, respect, courtesy, and fairness. I believe that these life's values were seeds that helped shape my life, especially perseverance.

I didn't know it at the time, but I believe learning to swim and overcoming fear helped shape my life. I was a shy little girl, unsure of myself, and often felt safer blending into the background than standing at the front. I was cautious, hesitant, afraid to make mistakes. I remember sitting in classrooms and hoped the teacher wouldn't call on me to read aloud so I often stayed quiet. I was content being with my friends and letting them be the leaders.

In the hot summer months my father, after a day of work, took my brothers and I to Lake Calhoun. My two years younger brother, Ralph, and I had to stay in the roped off area while Eugene (Gene later nick named "Andy" by his high school friends), who was six years older, could go out beyond the ropes because he could swim. I too wanted to do the same thing.

So in 1936 when I was 10, my parents signed me up for swimming lessons at the YWCA. Each week in the cold winter I would take the streetcar downtown for my lessons. At first, I was afraid of drowning and almost gave up. However, as the lessons continued and after much difficulty, I finally learned to swim.

There must have been something that would manifest confidence in me later because as a young child I pretended I was a tight ropewalker and climbed our clothes pole and tried to walk across the thin board that went from pole to pole. I fell off, and my shoe with a buttoned strap caught on the clothesline hook. I ended up hanging upside down by just the strap on one shoe. I yelled and my mother came running out to unhook me.

Another incident that makes me think my confidence was hiding was at Lake Washington in 1938 or 1939. For a number of years my father's friend offered to let our family use his cabin for the month of August. My younger brother, Ralph, and I met three boys who called themselves the "happy hollow gang" and I was also invited to belong.

The boys had set up a rope that hung from a middle tree between two others.

We would climb up a tree on the right, catch the rope and swing way to the left like Tarzan. One day while I was swinging, the rope broke and I fell and my head hit the ground. As I recall I think our attention turned to other escapades.

Like all girls in junior and high school we would earn extra money babysitting. But my first real job where I got a paycheck was at Sears Roebuck folding paper flyers that were to be sent out to customers. It was three hours after school and at first, I thought it was so boring but then I got an idea to accept the boring work and fold papers to the music in the background. When I got tired of that I decided to count how many I could do in 15 minutes which then led to counting how many in each half hour or hour. I've never forgotten about this job as I learned from it. If you don't like something, don't complain, accept it and find something about it to like. To this day I always look for something to like even if it is not my liking.

As I write this, the words perseverance and acceptance pop out at me. Evidently I had perseverance but didn't realize at the time I needed to accept it.

While I was in high school, a friend of mine talked me into joining her in a class to be a ballet swimmer in the Minneapolis Aqua follies during the July Aquatennial. Once again I found myself taking the streetcar in the cold winter months of 1942 to the University of Minnesota to practice.

This period of my life changed overnight along with our country. December 7, 1941, in Pearl Harbor Hawaii, 21 ships were bombed by Japan, 18 of which were lost and 2400 people lost their lives. Everyone's attention was turned to war. Almost every able bodied man and woman were joining a service to their country. Food and gas were rationed. If we wanted to buy gas, butter, flour, sugar, meat, or other staples, we had to use a stamp from our ration books. Even coal that heated our house was rationed. My father was in charge of blackouts in our area. However, I don't recall any threats.

My older brother joined the Army Signal Corps and ended up behind the front lines in Germany decoding messages of which he received the Bronze Star. 10 years later we finally got together. Many friends I knew from school never came back.

My boyfriend was killed in the Battle of Iwo Jima in March of 1945 which was extremely devastating to me, but I learned that you can't bring back people or circumstances. It is what it is, and we have to accept that. I still have the helpful book that my mother gave to me called, "Something to Live By" by Dorothea S. Kopplin, which was full of inspirational quotes from people in all walks of life and what they went through.

During this time, the feeling of inadequacy became more intense. I remember sitting on the bottom step of our stairway leading upstairs, hands on my face. My father approached me and asked, "What is wrong?"

I told him I'm just no good, I'm slow at learning and everything seems so difficult. I don't know where I'm going in life.

He simply said, "You learned to swim, didn't you?"

I can't explain it, but my attitude seemed to change. I thought about how hard it was to learn to swim and if I could do that maybe I could do more. I also remember a Bible quote from Matthew 9:29: It is done unto you as you believe.

Instead of dwelling on the negative, I decided to dwell on the things I had accomplished instead of what I thought I couldn't do. This change in my attitude helped alter my life. My father's question planted something in me that would grow and grow.

In spite of many closures, during the war, entertainment was not one of them. The troops and people needed to be uplifted, and the theme always had something positive about winning the war. Consequently, the Aqua Follies continued to be held in July of every year. I continued to take the streetcar each winter to practice at the University of Minnesota. I did this every year until the summer of 1945.

I took the money I had earned from appearing in the Aqua Follies and bought a train ticket to Richmond, California where my uncle Elmer, aunt Ione and their two girls, Dolores and Leone had moved to work in the shipyards. From there I visited my parent's friends in Los Angeles. While I was there, and since I was interested in doing something in the radio field, I had the opportunity to earn credits and enroll in the UCLA radio institute held at the NBC radio studios in Hollywood. This was 1946.

Just like a ripple in the water, one thing leads to another, including jobs. I worked as a waitress at a lunch counter, at a drug store, a beauty supply shop and at a flower shop along with going to school. Before I knew it, I was working in the radio field. I wasn't an on-air personality. I picked up little jobs here and there. This was a couple years before television came on the scene for the general public.

In the next few years I was married, moved to San Francisco, had two children, Danny and Janet, and was able to earn extra money through a modeling agency.

My marriage ended with an amiable departure. Through the agency, I worked at jobs offered by the conventions that came to town.

I demonstrated blow torches, hospital beds, business machines and all sorts of products. I was often offered a full time job with many of these companies. I think it was because, while demonstrating, I found reasons to believe in the product and was actually enthusiastic about them.

It was during this time I was sent out to a number of department stores in San Francisco on a project to demonstrate 45 record players which RCA Victor had just put on the market. At the same time Columbia Records came out with the 33 1/3 records.

While at the Emporium Department store a lady came up to me and asked, "Can I get Bing Crosby on 45 records?" I answered, "No, but you can get Perry Como, and he sounds just like him." She decided to buy the record player so I took her over to the salesperson and hoped she would be happy.

I was then approached by a fellow who had heard me and introduced himself as Les Malloy. Wow, he was a famous disc jockey in San Francisco. He told me he was starting a new television show at 4:30 in the afternoon and would like to talk to me about it. At that time television broadcasting began at six in the evening. His show would be at 4:30 to 6:00 in the late afternoon. I would be working for him, not the TV station. If I was interested, he would like to talk to me at KYA Radio where he was broadcasting.

I met him and he explained it would be an hour and a half, five-day-a-week interview and variety show, and we would be able to use the ABC radio 12- piece orchestra. My job would be to book the guests, appear on the show, and write up a few facts on each guest. The show would be live and ad lib, as tape for TV had not yet been developed. I would be his "Girl Friday" (today my title would be a co-host).

He then asked me, "Do you think you can do it?" I gulped, and said, "Ah ah yyes!"

He told me to call the Curran and Geary Theatres that booked stage plays and musicals and a few at the movie theaters because, in those days' movie stars came to town with their films and would speak and answer questions at intermissions. One of my first guests was Joan Crawford who was appearing in a movie and was in San Francisco to promote it.

And so, in the late 1949 began my career in television. Through those early years, I booked guests like Johnny Mathis, Phyllis Diller, Liberace, Perry Como, even the elderly Mr. JC Penny, before he died, and so many more stars as San Francisco were one of the top promotional cities.

In 1951 I got a call from Betty Jo Brown who said she had this guy who could do pushups through the entire 90 minute show. I immediately booked him because I could visualize the camera panning over to him every once in a while, while the show was going on. He never stopped for the entire 90 minutes. This led to his being asked to break the world record in pushups on the Art Baker "You Asked for It" national TV show. His name was Jack LaLanne.

The next thing I know about Jack LaLanne, he has his own show on KGO-TV at 9 a.m. *(Television began to shift from afternoon only shows to being on the air longer. Jack was to come on the 9:00 hour, after the kids' show Romper Room.)*

Jack LaLanne was a new phenomenon on the television tube. He insisted on only one camera so he could give exercises and pep talks to people as if they were in the same room. People were intrigued by his charisma, knowledge, and sincerity. The show took off like a freight train. Jack's mission, which became ours, was to help people help themselves.

I'll never forget the first day of the Jack LaLanne show. Jack talked to the TV like it was his best friend. All of us at the station watched the debut of this guy from Oakland.

Keep in mind, television shows and commercials were live. In fact, everything was live. Today, the only thing that is available to see about these early shows are still pictures.

Jack wanted to show the audience what bread does in the stomach. Not realizing the label was showing he took a loaf of white bread, took the wrapper off and squeezed the bread into a ball and threw it on the floor with a thud.

He said, "That's what happens with white bread in your stomach."

I thought it was funny and gulped. I recall gasping out loud, "Oh no. The wrapper. What's going to happen now?"

Showing the name on the wrapper was a no-no.

The sponsor called and told the station to get this guy off the air. After talks with the powers that be, he apologized, in as much as it was his first day and everyone realized television was so new, no one knew all the rules. In fact, a lot was trial and error.

Obviously, Jack was forgiven and allowed to continue. Eventually the show was syndicated nationwide for 34 years. Had he not been forgiven, I wouldn't be writing this today. Sometimes a simple act or word can change a life.

All shows were live in the early days so you had to be on your toes because nothing could be changed. It is what it is.

One example of how nothing could be changed is from my early days working with Les Malloy. Les and I were doing a commercial for a new car just on the market. Les was going on and on about the car and when he opened the door to show off the inside, the door fell off. I recall the crew had to take the doors off in order to get the car through the narrow door into the studio. The crew had put the door back but didn't attach it properly. They just laid the door in place not realizing Les would try to open it. But just like life you have to accept "what is."

As mentioned, everything was live. We had no scripts, it was all ad lib. I made a format of the guests and a few facts, maybe a sentence or two, about each one, then Les and I would reveal more about the person through the interview. After about four years, Les wanted to buy a radio station and turn it into a country and western format. He and his wife Georgene mortgaged their house and began a new career buying and selling radio stations.

So, inasmuch as I worked for him, not the TV station, I went to work in country and western radio. He had to start with new people. I learned to like country and western music. Les taught me how to write commercials. I can hear him say, "repeat repeat repeat." He taught me how to sell time on the station. He gave me my own radio show. I even learned to put the station on the air at five in the morning. I had to join the International Brotherhood of Electrical Workers of which I was the only woman member.

Les was a stellar salesman. One time he was trying to close a sale for a commercial for a very large company. But even the best salesman has a hard time getting all of the clients. So Les decided he would take a large box of fan mail, bundle it up and send it to the company. Within days, we got the commercial.

Les, like my dad, taught me perseverance. That word kept popping into my life and now it is a part of who I am!

Busy Life

My life was busy with the TV show and then running a radio station. Jack also had commitments to his 10,000 square foot Physical Culture Studio and his TV show. Plus, he lived in Alameda and I in South San

Francisco (40 miles apart), and being a mother, our time together was limited, the years seemed to fly by.

We flew to Las Vegas in 1959 and were married. Our son, Jon Allen came along in 1961, two years later.

CHAPTER 2

My Role as a Mother and in The Community

Backtracking to the Les Malloy show which was on from 4:30 to 6:00 Monday through Friday. I wanted Danny to become a Cub Scout. I found that all the dens were filled but if I would become a den mother, I could start another den of about six boys.

I volunteered!

I got off the air at 6:00 and my den meetings were held at 7:00. Often the little boys in the neighborhood would be waiting on my doorstep so I always had a project for them to show at the monthly meeting of all the dens.

Each week I would line up all the boys, each with an American flag and have them recite the Pledge of Allegiance. Janet, four years younger than Danny, felt left out so I let her join the boys. I would then have a project for the boys to work on. One of the projects we did was a flannel board that represented the American landscape in the song God Bless America. I had them sing it while each put on the flannel cut outs of the mountains and the prairies and the oceans white with foam. It was a hit at the monthly meeting of all the dens.

Danny participated in Boy Scouts all the way to the 12th grade and became a Sea Scout.

When Janet was old enough she became a Blue Bird and then went into Job's Daughters.

13 years later, Jon was old enough to join Cub Scouts. I called to have Jon join a den but once again the dens were all filled so I called the troop leader, and once again, volunteered.

The voice on the other end couldn't believe that I had called to volunteer. He took a deep breath and said, "I've been praying all night to find another den mother." It was TV's Kojak, Telly Savalas' brother, George. Jon's next door friend, Michael, wanted to join too, so his mother, Michele Boyer volunteered to help me. Just by volunteering, it made me happy, Michele happy, George happy, the boys in the den happy and the monthly meetings of all the dens were happy. Example: The ripple effect.

For three years Michele and I were co-den mothers. We've both moved on but to this day, she in her early 90s and me 100, are still close friends and keep in touch frequently.

A Pat on the Back

In 1961 I joined WAIF, an organization started by Jane Russell after WWll. She had adopted an unwanted homeless child from Europe after the war and saw a need to raise money to put these unwanted children in adoptive homes. Four years later after joining, I found myself Ball Chairman for an event. Jane and our committee invited Queen Elizabeth's sister, Princess Margaret and Lord Snowden as our guests of honor. They accepted.

It was a monumental undertaking with all the protocol but a huge success with 1500 people in attendance which made money so that children could be placed in loving homes.

The next year I was asked to take on the position of president but didn't have the time. I did accept the position in 1967 and with the help of Jane's notoriety, The King and Queen of Thailand accepted to be our guests. This also was a huge success. I enlisted Janet and Yvonne, (Jack's daughter from his prior marriage) to help sell raffle tickets during the event. Janet and Yvonne eventually went on to volunteer for their particular charity events.

When you work with a lot of people everyone has their own ideas of how and where the event should take place. I had a way of trying to consider everyone. When people would complain personally to me, and there would be different stories, then I would have a meeting with everyone involved. When we put everything on the table, complaints were few and far between.

Being in this position helped me learn to be accepting and even-keeled when it comes to working with others. Eventually everything comes to fruition when we have patience and perseverance.

The next few years, our fundraisers turned to booking ships overnight where we could go out to sea beyond the perimeter where it was legal to gamble. We would book rooms on the ship and guests would stay overnight. The press was also invited. Some members of the press wouldn't like their room and would complain. The committee members would send me to talk to them. So I would find a room that wasn't as convenient and suggest, enthusiastically, they try that room. To me, it wasn't as good as the original room, but it seemed to make them happy.

Sometimes, the press would arrive late and found that someone had taken their seat. Instead of rearranging the seats, I would enthusiastically suggest that Jack and I had a great table (which was in the back of the room) and they could sit with us.

It all boils down to people needing a pat on the back. I try to make people feel special and appreciated for what they are doing.

Golf and the Sand Trap

Despite all the extra activities I found time to play golf as that was really my enjoyment.

Let me tell you a story about golf and what can be learned from it. Anyone who's played knows you can't take the shot over. It's just like life, you can't change anything after it has happened. I think it is one of the reasons I could get through the death of my daughter in an auto accident when she had just turned 21.

I was in a tournament and doing very well and near the end if I continued to play well, if I could hold on, I could win. The last hole my shot to the green landed in the sand trap. As I approached the ball in the sand, I thought, "What if I miss this shot?"

I did! In fact, I got so frustrated I missed the next shot.

I then said to myself, "I'm going to put this shot up to the pin."

I did! That opened my eyes. Something told me to think about putting the shot next to the pin and I did. The lesson here is that my thoughts made it happen. If you think you can't, you can't. If you think you can, you can. Simple as that. You have to believe in yourself!

Jack would often quip there was no exercise in following the little ball around. He ended up taking up golf with me and became a golf-a-holic. We would sometimes play 36 holes in one day. Jack ended up having a motto about golf: When I play, I play for keeps and tear the grass in great big heaps.

Chapter 3

My First Date with Jack LaLanne

Let me backtrack to just before Les Malloy left TV to buy the radio station.

Jack and a couple of his buddies would come into the TV studio often to watch the show and then go to dinner. Jack would ask me to join them, but I would turn him down.

One day when asked to go to dinner with Jack's two buddies and their wives, I accepted. While waiting for our table at a new restaurant called Doros we had to wait about 30 minutes, so we went next door to a piano bar. As we walked in, the pianist knew Jack and called him over and asked him to sing. He knew Jack had a beautiful singing voice. In fact, Jack at one time wanted to be an opera singer. He sang Mario Lanza's "Because You're Mine." I, along with other customers, were impressed, and I even exclaimed, "He can sing too?"

But it wasn't his singing that impressed me as much as his philosophy of life. During our conversations that evening, I felt I really got to really know him. I became intrigued with his brain and how he looked at life which corresponded with my beliefs.

In those days, the movies made muscle men look like they didn't have much upstairs. I discovered that our minds were on the same level. We had a meeting of the minds. I was attracted to his way of thinking especially when he said, "Your mind is a mine, full of diamonds and all you need to do is dig them up!" He also had a wonderful sense of humor full of funny one liners!

That was the beginning of our friendship and relationship, with dinners from time to time and seeing each other more often as time permitted.

As mentioned, we were both very busy with our lives. Thank goodness for my neighbors, Aggie and Tony Hogh and their two daughters, Karen and Carolyn, for helping me take care of my kids.

Jack wanted me to work for him, but I had to fulfill my obligation to Les. Once the radio station got under way, I left and went to work for Jack.

What began as a professional connection soon became a personal one.

Our first dates were about vision. We talked about health, about discipline, about making people stronger in body and spirit. It wasn't just love at first sight – it was purpose at first sight. Jack and I were on the same page, he had the ideas and knowledge through his love of the book *Grey's Anatomy*, his Chiropractic degree and many years as a gym owner.

Our marriage was often described as a partnership – and it was. It was built on love, respect, and belief in one another. We were often asked what makes our marriage work. We both answered, "Because we're friends too!"

Chapter 4

The Business

Jack had rented an office in Oakland, below his 10,000 square foot Physical Culture Studio.

The first thing I did was change the lock on the door, as the products he was selling on TV were slowly disappearing.

I took over his financial books, paid the bills and ordered a product that was made for him by Mel Williamson, his student and biochemist.

I was not with Jack when he created his nutrition line. His first product was Pro 60 and Pro 70 Protein tablets which led the way to other products.

Jack came up with the ideas. I helped carry them out. He was against gimmicks to sell a product. He had to believe in it and actually use it. Selling products is how we were able to stay on the air and nationally syndicate the shows. All through trial and error.

There were no national exercise shows. There were very few exercise shows in smaller markets, but Jack's show, I feel, opened the door to the fitness industry as it is today. But to keep the door open we had to sell products to pay for television airtime.

Two of the prominent products we developed that opened that door in the middle 1950s include a stretch band which we called the Glamour Stretcher and Instant Breakfast protein drink.

It was so popular and sold so many that we were able to move our office to Los Angeles and hired Hank Akerberg as our General Manager.

This led to marketing the product through the Jack LaLanne Show which was eventually syndicated.

I mentioned earlier that Jack's first show in San Francisco took off like a freight train; the same thing happened nationwide.

Jack made sense, he was sincere and believed from his heart. It wasn't just words he was speaking, his words had deep, life-changing meaning. He sincerely wanted to "help people help themselves" to a healthier life. I understand this because I was a junk food junkie and didn't know it until I met Jack.

During the time when I was doing the late afternoon show with Les Malloy, one day, I came into the newsroom early with my usual chocolate donut and cigarette in hand. I went to my desk and started working. Jack's show was set to air at 9:00 am. Jack walked back to my desk and said, "You really should be eating apples, bananas, oranges and natural foods."

So I responded by taking a puff of my cigarette and blew smoke in his face and said, "OH Yeah, REALLY?"

Interestingly, Jack was going to do a pep talk segment on his show called "The dangers of smoking." Jack had colored pictures of a black lungs, holey lungs and pink lungs. Seeing these pictures scared me. I knew about people who had trouble breathing, but I didn't know it was the result of smoking. Back then a lot of new data was coming out!

I quit smoking immediately and started consuming Kevoettes, an appetite appeaser instead of cigarettes, which was one of the sponsors of his show.

As Jack would say "It was one nail OUT of her coffin."

On that same day Jack's brother, Norman, burst through the studio newsroom door saying, "Hey Jack, I just quit smoking and did you know my lungs were black? It takes a whole year to get the tar and nicotine out of your lungs!"

That's it, I said to myself. I'm never going to have another cigarette again. I don't want black and holey lunges. I don't want to be old when I'm old.

So I went from a junk-food-junkie to a non-smoker and living a healthy, vibrant life after meeting Jack.

When I went to work for Jack, I was thankful for the opportunities I had in radio and television with Les Malloy. I had the knowledge to help set up his personal appearances, lectures, national TV shows and interviews.

People give me credit for his success which I can't take. Les Malloy taught me a lot but Jack taught me about what exercise can do for the body; what food to put in my mouth. He gave me confidence that I could also do lectures.

One day Jack told me, "I'm going to LA as I have an opportunity to go on KTTV, Channel 11."

As I was taking him to the airport, he reminded me that he had lectures scheduled that I had set up. He said, "I can't do them. You'll have to do them. And you'll have to do the show in San Francisco, too."

In my shocked and nervous voice, I replied, "I can't do your show, and I can't do your lectures! I have no idea how to do lectures!"

He said only one sentence that changed my attitude and confidence: "If you know your subject you can talk about it."

I did his shows and lectures that were on the docket. I was scared stiff. But he was right. I knew the subject. Surprisingly to me, the people loved it.

He also taught me that if I was enthusiastic about it I could do it. Through this I got more confident.

With his new show in LA and me in San Francisco with no tape or film, we had to do each show live in both places. I did one week in San Francisco and then flew down to LA to do the show there. Jack would be the opposite. He would do the show in LA for a week and then fly to San Francisco for a week. We did this for several months until we were able to film the shows. Then we started to syndicate the shows in different markets, starting with New York and Philadelphia.

As the years rolled by Jack did more and more lectures around the country. He was electric on stage with his ad lib lectures. I warmed up the audience, gave my transformation story into fitness and introduced him.

After his lecture I would ask the audience, "How many people believe Jack believes?" Enthusiastically, everyone would raise their hands.

I would then ask, "How would you like to hear Jack sing "I Believe?" The audience would raise their hands but not as enthusiastically.

Jack would sing "I Believe" acapella, right on key. The audience was stunned and on its feet immediately. I often joked to him, "You didn't want to sing but that's how you get your standing ovations!"

You can see by these little incidents in our life that Jack and I were a team working together which I believe became part of each of our legacies. He had the ideas, I ran with them. He started the motor and with his advice, I put my foot on the gas pedal. My advice to you here is that if you are starting a new project, you can't just turn the key, you have to put your foot on the gas pedal.

Seeds That Grow Beyond Us

I don't think I'd be alive today if Jack hadn't come into my life. I never realized that his influence would be a seed that would grow my own legacy. Jack had vision, charisma, and an unshakable determination to bring fitness into every home in America. My energy complimented his energy, and we both had the ability to connect with people heart-to-heart. Our seeds were not just in the fitness world, but in the lives of everyday people who discovered that movement and self-care could transform their futures. My legacy is not only tied to Jack's. It is my own.

Your Legacy, Too

I look back now and realize that my father's simple question carried more wisdom than I could have known as a little girl: "You learned to swim, didn't you?"

Yes, I did. And from that moment on, I understood – sometimes the smallest victories carry the greatest weight. They are the beginnings of legacies.

So, as you are reading this book, as you hear not only my stories but the stories of many others who have been part of this journey, I hope you'll see this truth: **you have a legacy too.** It may start with something small. But if you persevere it will grow into something remarkable.

Chapter 5

Love, Legacy, and Shared Vision

More Than Feats

Many people remember Jack for his headline feats of strength (which are well documented in my book *Pride and Discipline*). The purpose of these feats was to prove what the body is capable of doing.

The first I remember was in 1954. I hadn't been dating Jack very long and was invited to view his underwater swim underneath the Golden Gate Bridge. With 140 pounds in two air tanks on his back, he was lowered into the water on the San Rafael side of the Golden Gate Bridge to swim underwater to the San Francisco side of the bridge. Mission accomplished with just a few breaths of air in the tanks.

Jack would say, "If I can do these feats, certainly you could at least spend a few minutes taking care of your God-given body."

These feats were impressive, yes – but they weren't just for show. Jack was showing the world what the human body and mind were capable of when fueled by purpose. The purpose was to show if he could do these feats.

More Than Muscles

People saw and were awed by his feats, but they saw more than that. They saw and felt his charisma, his honesty, sincerity, determination and follow through. They saw Jack swimming handcuffed, ankles shackled, across San Francisco Bay, towing boats behind him. They saw him knocking out fingertip push-ups with the flair of a magician. But what they didn't always see was the planning, preparation, and the long nights of logistics that went into those events.

If he dreamed it, I wanted to ensure every detail was in place – from safety protocols to press releases to making sure we captured the moment.

The Behind-the-Scenes Partner

When he was invited to speak, I coordinated travel and schedules. I made sure the message never got lost in the hype. People might have come to see the feats, but what mattered most was the lesson behind them: discipline, resilience, and believing that you can do more than you think.

His presentations were ad-libbed, inspirational and funny. We were a team. I warmed up the audience with a short story about my transformation from a smoker and junk food junkie and had the audience do some simple exercises. After I introduced him, I jumped into his arms and as he caught me, he came up with another funny one liner. His presentations always began with a joke.

If you want to inspire people, you can't just tell them – you have to show them. You have to package the message in a way that captures their imagination and stays in their memory.

We made the press curious to secure coverage. Jack might have been able to swim while shackled, but without a story to frame it, the message could be lost. Together, we built living parables about what the human body and mind can accomplish.

Shaping the Message

Jack had more ideas in an hour than most people had in a lifetime. My job was to help channel those ideas.

When we wrote books, Jack's voice poured passionately onto the page. I would help refine it, edit, and organize it.

All the books we each wrote were from our heart to the reader's heart.

The same was true with our operations. While Jack trained, taught, and performed, I handled contracts, the media relations, the calls with producers and publishers and managed schedules, booked appearances.

Belief is the Business Model of Jack's name

Jack's brand is his belief!

Today, people talk about branding, marketing, or influence. Back then, we didn't call it that – we just lived it. But looking back, I see that the basis of our business wasn't just fitness, television, or books. It was the belief that people mattered, that discipline could transform a life, and that people have extraordinary potential inside them.

At the heart of everything we did was belief. Not marketing strategy. Not financial gain. Just belief.

That belief became our business model. When Jack opened his gyms, they weren't just places with weights and machines. They were classrooms of belief. When he spoke on television, he wasn't just demonstrating exercises – he was planting seeds of belief and trust in living rooms across America.

Belief was Jack's way of positive thinking. It was his mantra. He would not tolerate negative thinking in our household. He would always say, "We don't talk negative in this house."

I am positive that Jack was able to accomplish his feats because of this attitude.

Chapter 6

My Philosophy of Fitness

Jack always said, *"Your body is your slave. It works for you."* I took that to heart. I believe that what you put in your mouth, how much you move, and how you think – that's your true fitness formula. I've learned to treat my body like a best friend and my mind like a powerful ally.

What Fitness is to Me

Fitness, to me, has never been complicated. The world seems to make it complicated – diets with fancy names, gadgets that promise shortcuts, and workouts that sound like rocket science. But the truth is simple: it's how you think, how you move, and what you put in your mouth!

Food is Fuel

Food is not just about flavor – it's about fuel. Jack preached this long before it was popular. He promoted juicing in the 1930s, when most people thought "health food" meant cottage cheese and prunes.

I learned from him, but I also lived it in my own way. Jack often would exclaim, "What you eat today is walking and talking tomorrow."

Motion is Life

I was recently interviewed by Danielle Friedman of the New York Times about my life and fitness. At some point during the interview, I happened to say "if you don't move, you become immoveable." The editors got a kick out of it so they left it in the article. It's a silly expression, but it's true.

Motion is life, and life is motion. The body is not meant to sit still. It is designed to bend, stretch, lift, walk, run, twist, and dance.

My own routines are simple. I probably spend 20-30 minutes a day really making my muscles work hard. I lift weights. I stretch. I never miss doing 20-30 Jack knife sit-ups every morning. Sometimes I walk on the treadmill. I'm training for life. Movement keeps the joints supple, the muscles strong, and the circulation flowing.

And the best part? You don't have to do what I do. You don't have to lift dumbbells or knock out sit-ups. You just have to move.

Walk your dog. Plant your garden. Dance in your kitchen. Sometimes I hold onto the sink and do leg lifts or pushups against the sink. Fitness is about a lifestyle of movement.

The Power of Thought

Your mind is the steering wheel of your life. If it's filled with negativity, excuses, and fear, you will drive yourself into a ditch. But if it's filled with gratitude, possibility, and discipline, you will drive yourself toward health, joy, and purpose.

I've learned to treat my mind like a powerful ally. That means feeding it good positive things. I surround myself with people who uplift me. I practice gratitude like it's a muscle.

You can exercise every day and eat perfectly, but if your thoughts are toxic, you will never feel whole. Fitness is not just about the body – it's about the mind and spirit. And when those three align, that's when you feel truly alive.

So here it is, plain and simple:

- **Fuel your body wisely.**
- **Move it daily.**
- **Feed your mind with positivity.**

That's it. That's the philosophy. And if you live it, I promise you will not just add years to your life, but life to your years.

Chapter 7

Continuing the Mission

When Jack passed, I knew his mission couldn't end. I continued our work, speaking, writing, and sharing our story with new generations. I still hear his voice in my head: *"Help people help themselves. And what you've learned, pass it on."* That's what I've done, and what I'll continue to do.

The Day Everything Changed

Losing Jack was one of the hardest moments of my life. For decades, we had been a team. Suddenly, I had to face the world without the man who had been my partner in every sense of the word.

But here's the truth: while I lost Jack's physical presence, I never lost his voice. I can still hear him, as clear as ever, reminding me of the principles we lived by: discipline, consistency, perseverance, joy, and service to others. And in that way, Jack has never left me.

Passing It On

As mentioned before, Jack's favorite phrases were, *"Help people help themselves,"* and *"What you've learned, pass it on."*

That's why I've dedicated myself to mentoring younger voices in the fitness and wellness world through the "LaLanne Pass It On" podcast with myself and Greg Justice.

When I see the passion in their eyes – the same passion Jack carried – I know the flame is still alive. I like it when people ask me questions. When I'm interviewed, I don't think there's a question that I can't answer when it comes to living life. When someone asks me something, I'm positive about it to help them do the same. I know the message will not fade, because it's being carried forward by a new generation of believers.

Reaching New Generations

It amazes me that even today, young people who never saw *The Jack LaLanne Show* still know Jack's name. They've heard of his feats, they've seen clips online, or they've read quotes and have seen the juicer commercials. But there are those who have never heard of him.

I knew I wanted to keep carrying the flame. I wanted to make sure Jack got is due and what he's contributed to fitness. Young people need to see that health, energy, and joy are possible for a lifetime.

Chapter 8

What I've Learned

I've learned to forgive myself. To laugh. To take care of my health account like I would my bank account. I've learned that muscles need movement, that excuses are well-planned pardons, and that thoughts – good or bad – become things, so I choose to think positive.

The Freedom of Forgiveness

One of the most powerful lessons of my life has been learning to forgive – especially myself. When you live a long life, you're bound to make mistakes. I've stumbled, said the wrong thing, missed opportunities, or let people down. For years, I carried those moments like weights. But the longer I lived, the more I realized: you can't move forward if you're always dragging yesterday behind you.

Forgiving myself didn't mean ignoring mistakes. It meant learning from them, then letting them go. Forgiveness freed me to keep moving – not just physically, but emotionally and spiritually.

The Healing Power of Laughter

I've learned that laughter is medicine. Jack and I laughed every single day, even in the tough seasons. Humor carried us through challenges, long days on the road, even moments when things didn't go as planned. He always had a one liner that had me burst into laughter.

A normal dinner conversation would come around to a one-liner about his fitness philosophy - he lived it, breathed it, and ate it.

There's a reason they say laughter is the best medicine – it lowers stress, lifts your spirit, and connects you to others.

Even now, I look for reasons to laugh every day. Sometimes at myself, sometimes with friends, sometimes at the little absurdities of life. If you can laugh, you can live.

Your Health Account

Jack always professed, "Your health account and your bank account are synonymous. The more you put in, the more you can take out."

Every choice you make is a deposit or a withdrawal. Movement, healthy food, rest, gratitude – those are deposits. Junk food, stress, excuses, neglect – those are withdrawals.

Just like with money, you can't keep making withdrawals without eventually going bankrupt. I've met people who spent decades neglecting their health, thinking they could make up for it later. But the truth is, health debt comes due, and often the cost is higher than you expected.

The good news is, it's never too late to start making deposits. Every walk, stretch, and vegetable on your plate is an investment in your future self. I didn't "diet" or "exercise." I invested. That investment has paid dividends in energy, vitality, and longevity.

Making these investments can't come with excuses.

Jack used to say, "Excuses are well-planned pardons." He was right. Excuses are the stories we tell ourselves to avoid discomfort. "I don't have time." "I'm too tired." "I'll start tomorrow." I've used them, too. We all have.

Jack and I would often answer in unison, "Think of the results."

That line stuck with me. When I felt like I wanted to eat more or I didn't want to exercise, I just needed to think of the results.

Can't get motivated to invest in yourself? You eat every day. How do you get motivated to brush your teeth? You have to leave the house, how do you get motivated to put your shoes on?

Thoughts Become Things

Perhaps the most important lesson I've learned is that thoughts – good or bad – become things. Your thoughts shape your actions, your actions shape your habits, and your habits shape your life.

Your thoughts are like seeds. What you plant will grow.

That's why I choose positive thoughts. Not because life is always easy, but because positivity gives me strength to handle the hard times. Gratitude, laughter, and belief are the fertilizers of a healthy mind. And a healthy mind is the foundation of a healthy life.

When I put all these lessons together, I see a picture of what it means to live well:

- Forgive yourself and others.
- Laugh often.
- Treat your health like a bank account.
- Keep your muscles – and your mind – in motion.
- Stop making excuses.
- Choose positive thoughts.

If I had to sum up the lessons of my life, it would be this: life is short, but it is also abundant.

Chapter 9

I Don't Want to be Old When I'm Old

One morning on Jack's show, he proclaimed, *"The power of movement is your motor, your generator of life. If you don't move, you atrophy and wither away. Yet, you can actually reverse the aging process; it's like a sport; you have to train for it."*

70+ years ago when I was about 27, I thought I was old because I was nearing 30.

Jack's words resonated with me. I didn't want to be old when I was old. So I quit smoking and started to train using Jack's exercise program. I ate live, vital food instead of the junk food I was consuming (including candy bars for lunch!)

I will be 100 when this book is published, and I'm often asked how I've lived this long.

Most people grow up with a picture of aging that looks like decline: more pills, less movement, fewer dreams. It's almost as if society has written a script that suggests once you hit a certain age, your best days are behind you, or says, "You're too old for that."

But I've lived long enough to know that script is wrong.

Aging doesn't have to mean slowing down. That's what I call *The LaLanne Way.*

Joy is the first marker of aging well. Joy is something practiced, but happiness is something that comes and goes.

When you're younger, it's easy to confuse joy with happiness. But with age, you learn that joy is simpler and deeper. It's in the morning stretch that loosens your body or the laughter you share with a friend or simply being grateful for waking up to another day.

I've learned that the older you get, the more joy matters. It's the reason I still laugh at myself and find humor in the little things.

One story comes to mind. When I was working with the Les Malloy show in San Francisco, a friend and I were going up an escalator one weekend talking and laughing about something. Another lady was coming down the escalator and asked as we passed each other, "Are you Elaine?" I said, "Yes. How do you know?" As we passed each other and she was continuing down the escalator, she yelled back, "I recognize your laugh!"

My fine lines are my laugh lines and part of my personality. I have found that people like you for your inner self, not your outer self. So go spread some joy.

Wisdom That Only Comes With Time

Wisdom is the second marker of aging well. It comes from mistakes made and lessons learned, and from years of showing up – through storms, through victories, through ordinary days.

At 99, I've learned to be more curious about things. Curiosity doesn't erase years; it keeps you growing and moving forward. Nobody wants to sit with someone who only talks about the past. But sit with someone who is curious about the present and the future? That's inspiring.

Take for instance, our newsletter. I was curious about where the word July came from. I decided to look up the word. I found out it was connected to Julius Caesar, and it took me down a path of looking up more and more. It's been exciting to deeply learn more about the meaning of words. I've always been curious, but I never took the time to investigate those curiosities. I'm so glad I did. I've realized wisdom is not about having all the answers. It's about being curious.

And wisdom, once earned, is meant to be shared. Wisdom multiplies when it's passed on.

Contribution as the Crown

Nothing keeps you young like giving of yourself. When you contribute you step outside of yourself and into purpose.

Jack always said, "Living is giving." He was right. Contribution keeps you connected. It reminds you that you're part of something bigger than your own limitations.

For me, contribution has meant carrying our message, inspiring others to take ownership of their health, and modeling what vitality can look like at any age.

Aging is a process and a progress that we cannot change but can slow it down.

I believe aging has three dimensions: Chronological, Mental and Physical.

CHRONOLOLOGICAL AGE:

My actual age IS NOT important to me.

MENTAL AGE:

My mental age IS important to me. I think young, visualize I'm young, dwell on the positive, toss out the negative and I enjoy people who have a great sense of humor. Jack and I laughed through our life together. Neither one of us liked discord, so he made fun out of almost everything.

There is no set age at which we must slow down. Don't fret about it. If you think you're old, YOU ARE!

PHYSICAL AGE:

I strive to keep my physical age young by a simple exercise routine.

You eat every day, you sleep every day, your body was made to move every day.

If you and I were having a one-on-one conversation I would tell you about my acronym:

A R C H: Attitude, Resistance, Consistency, Harmony.

A – ATTITUDE: Have a positive attitude, and look at the bright side of everything, no matter the circumstance.

Life often gives us setbacks we're not expecting, and we can't seem to see the light at the end of the tunnel, including me. I believe we must accept those setbacks.

Losing our daughter in an auto accident at the young age of 21, I could have chosen to have a long pity party for myself or accept that I could not bring her back. I can't bring Jack back. I choose to accept and concentrate on wonderful memories. I know in my heart both would want me to go on to help others.

So if you feel negative, practice sweeping negative thoughts out with positive ones; it works!

R – RESISTANCE: The key element in building and toning a muscle. This is also the premise of weight training and resistance bands.

Muscles get weak with inactivity. Strengthen them with exercise and stretch for flexibility. Maintain elasticity of your ligaments and tendons.

Equally, RESIST the foods that are undermining your health. A healthy bloodstream is your River of Life.

C – CONSISTENCY: Be consistent in your workouts and eating habits. Jack advocated: *"It's not what you do SOME of the time that counts! It's what you do MOST of the time that counts!"*

A consistent exercise and good nutrition program give you more strength and energy; it's your personal insurance policy.

H – HARMONY: Balance within your mind and body creates peace, confidence, and harmony within you.

If you live with a positive **Attitude**, practice **Resistance** and be Con-sistent, you end up with balanced **Harmony** in your life.

Never Too Old to Grow

The phrase "you can't teach an old dog new tricks" has always made me laugh. It's simply not true. I've reinvented myself many times – television host, producer, wife, mom, fitness advocate, author, speaker.

The secret is staying open-minded. Growth doesn't stop when you turn 50, 70, or 90. In fact, some of the most profound growth happens later, because you've finally gathered enough wisdom to put the pieces together.

The LaLanne Way

So what is *The LaLanne Way* of aging? It's simple:

- **Move daily.** Keep your body in motion, because movement is life.

- **Think positively.** Train your brain as faithfully as you train your muscles.

- **Eat wisely.** Food is fuel – choose the kind that keeps you strong.

- **Laugh often.** Humor lightens the load of age.

- **Give freely.** Contribution turns years into legacy.

- **Stay curious.** Curiosity keeps you young at heart.

It's not a complicated formula, but it works. It's carried me through a century of life with vim, vigor and vitality.

Chapter 10

The Mind-Body Connection – My Inner Strength

Everything starts in your mind. I've seen firsthand how negative thinking can sabotage even the strongest body. That's why I train my brain like I train my muscles. Visualizing success has helped me overcome fear, self-doubt, and even sand traps on the golf course.

The Battlefield of the Mind

I've always believed that the greatest battles we face aren't fought with our bodies – they're fought in our minds. You can be strong as an ox, with muscles that turn heads, but if your thoughts are filled with doubt, fear, or negativity, those muscles won't carry you far. The mind drives the body. And if the mind quits, the body follows.

I've watched people talk themselves out of opportunities before they ever took the first step. They said, "I can't," and their bodies obeyed. I've done it myself at times – hesitated, doubted, let fear creep in. But I learned quickly that the thoughts we repeat become the reality we live. If you believe you can't, you won't. If you believe you can, your body will rise to the occasion.

Chapter 11

My Books, and the One I Didn't Plan

I didn't think I could write. I thought everyone else was better. But at 60, I wrote my first book. It seems my life took a change at 60. Since then, I've written seven. But the book I didn't plan – the life I've lived – is my greatest story.

Doubting My Voice

For a long time, I didn't believe I had anything worth writing. I admired other authors. They seemed to have eloquence, and their words seemed to leap off the page with confidence and grace. Compared to them, my voice felt small.

I told myself, *You're not a writer. You're an organizer, a doer, a supporter. Leave the words to someone else.*

But stories were building inside me. I just didn't think anyone would want to hear them.

The Leap at 60

Then came a turning point at 60 years old. I finally said yes to writing my first book.

That book became a beginning, and when it was published, something amazing happened. People read it! They connected with it. They told me my words encouraged them.

It was proof that you don't have to be perfect to be impactful. You just have to be willing.

Seven Books, Seven Pieces of Me

Each one of my books is like a chapter of my fitness journey and a little about my life.

Fitness After 50 was my first book focused on fitness and health. Richard Benyo, a former publisher of Runner's world magazine, was my co-author who talked me into doing this first book.

Next came *Dynastride* - a book about walking. I noticed that some people just walk, they don't put any energy into their walk. *Dynastride*, a term Jack coined, put energy into your walk by purposely swinging your arms and taking a good stride.

The third book was one of my favorites, *Fitness after 50 Workout*. The reason I had this idea is because a lot of times when you're working out and making your program, sometimes you can't remember all the exercises. This book includes exercises from head to toe in succession; for your mind, eyes, face, neck, all the way down to your toes.

Book four was a recipe book, *Eating Right for a New You*. It included my own recipes and those from good friends.

I also wrote *Total Juicing*, a recipe book on juicing and its benefits.

If you want to Live, Move: Putting the Boom Back in Boomers with Jaime Brenkus was the next book. Jaime called our agent, Rick Hersh, wanting to partner with me on a book. Our motto of this book was that eight minutes a day gets you on your way.

Pride and Discipline: The Legacy of Jack LaLanne is my most recent book. In this book we highlight Jack's writings about the mind and a strong desire to live and be active, eat live, vital foods and practice positive thoughts. It is a timeless guide to living a strong, purposeful life.

Every book is different, but they all had something in common: they came from my heart. I realized writing isn't about competing with others; it's more about contribution and leaving something behind that says, *This is what I learned. This is what I've lived. Maybe it can help you too.*

It's Never Too Late

If there's one message I want people to take from my journey as an author, it's never too late. I was 60 when I started.

So if you've ever thought, *It's too late for me,* I'm here to tell you: it isn't.

Don't worry about whether you're "good enough" to write a book, or build a legacy, or live a meaningful life. Just speak or write from your heart.

Chapter 12

My Simple Truths

Life boils down to three things: how you think, what you eat, and how much you move. That's it. I keep things simple because life is too short to complicate.

The Power of Simplicity

We live in a world that loves to complicate things. Every week there's a new diet, a new workout craze, a new app that promises the secret to health and happiness. But after nearly a century of living, I can tell you with certainty: the basics still work.

What you need is a mindset that lifts you up, food that fuels you, and movement that keeps you strong. That's it. That's the formula.

The Legacy of Simplicity

If you want to know my "secret" to living well:

- **Guard your thoughts.** Choose positivity.
- **Fuel your body.** Eat foods that give you life.
- **Keep moving.** Every day, in every way you can.

The Power of Passing It On

The phrase *"pass it on"* has become something of a mantra for me. It's simple, but it carries power.

- If you've learned to forgive, pass it on.
- If you've discovered strength, pass it on.
- If you've found laughter in hard times, pass it on.
- If you've chosen gratitude over bitterness, pass it on.
- If you've lived through storms and come out stronger, pass it on.
- If you have curiosity, pass it on.
- Life is great when you're in shape: mentally, physically and spiritually.
- If you have perseverance in life and accept life as it is and have a sense of humor, you've got it made.

Chapter 13

My Legacy, Your Legacy

Life has shown that legacy isn't about fame, money, or headlines. Legacy is about impact. Impact doesn't require a spotlight – it requires consistency.

You're building it every day in the way you treat people, in the choices you make, in the love you share.

The more I lived, the more I realized legacy is woven into the smallest moments.

I never set out to be the "First Lady of Fitness." That title came much later, and it wasn't one I felt fit me. It was given to me by the people in the industry and the press. What I set out to do was simple: support a mission I believed in, live with purpose, and love with all my heart.

If there's a formula for legacy, it's not complicated. For me, it comes down to three things:

- **Intention** means living on purpose.
- **Honesty** means being true to yourself and others.
- **Heart** means showing up with love.

Those three ingredients have shaped every season of my life. And I believe they are available to anyone, anywhere.

The Ripples We Create

Legacy is not just what you leave behind – it's what you pass forward while you're still here. It's the ripple effect of your actions. I think about the people I've met along the way – the mothers who told me our television show inspired them to exercise with their kids, the trainers who built careers because they were influenced by Jack's philosophies, the younger women who said my energy gave them hope for their own later years. Those are the ripples. And the best part? You don't always get to see the ripples. Sometimes your impact reaches places you'll never know.

As I think back to my life, I feel that my legacy is one of **perseverance**, **acceptance**, and a good **sense of humor**. I've persevered through every little challenge and accepted the outcomes, often using humor.

So the question isn't whether you'll leave a legacy – you will. The question is: *what kind of legacy will it be?*

PART 2:

Her Legacy

Introduction: Carrying the Flame Together

Legacy is not built in isolation. It's not a solo performance or a one-person stage. Legacy is built in community, carried forward by the people whose lives have been touched, changed, and inspired along the way.

Elaine "LaLa" LaLanne has shared her story in these pages with honesty, humor, and heart. We've walked through her early years of discovery, her partnership with Jack, her philosophy of fitness and life, and the lessons she has gathered over nearly a century of living with intention. But as powerful as her story is, it is not the end of the book – it is the beginning of something bigger.

Elaine's legacy has never been just her own. It has always been about the ripple effect. One act of encouragement sparks another. One story of resilience inspires someone else to rise. One life of consistency shows countless others what's possible. HER Legacy isn't a single voice – it's a chorus.

That's what this next section is about.

Here, you'll hear from leaders, friends, family members, and visionaries whose lives have been impacted by Elaine, Jack, and the values they embodied together. Each voice will bring its own perspective. Some will share stories of working alongside her. Others will reflect on how her example shaped their path. Still others will speak about how they've carried similar truths into their own fields of influence.

The beauty of legacy is that it multiplies. Elaine's life reminds us that one person's courage to live with integrity can create opportunities for others to do the same. In that way, legacy is both personal and collective. It begins in one life, but it doesn't stay there. It carries forward – through us, through you, through the generations to come.

As you turn these pages, you'll see HER Legacy come alive in many forms. You'll hear how discipline shaped careers, how laughter sustained friendships, how presence changed families, and how integrity built platforms that endure. And perhaps, as you read, you'll begin to recognize the threads of your own legacy, already being woven through your life.

Because the truth is this: HER Legacy is not only Elaine's. It's not only the stories of those who contribute to this book. HER Legacy is an invitation – for all of us to live with the kind of purpose, joy, and faithfulness that leaves something lasting behind.

So, let's carry the flame together.

Chapter 14

Wrong Way. Go Back.

By Keli Roberts

Growing up in Australia in the 60's and 70's in a broken family, I relied heavily on my love of playing sports, especially swimming. From the age of six I was a competitive swimmer, and my love of the water got me through a troubled childhood. My parents were divorced by the time I turned seven, and I was glad my father and all the violence was gone. For the time being, Mum remarried and for a couple of years things were stable and happy, but that was not for long. My stepfather committed suicide and again my family life was in turmoil. The only comfort I found was my love of swimming.

In my early pre-teens, I was molested by a friend of the family, and I didn't have a secure relationship with my mother to rely on her to help me sort through the complicated feelings it brought up. In school, I never felt like I fit in. I felt like an outsider. Fortunately, I was an outstanding swimmer and that built my fractured self-esteem, and I channeled all my hurt and pain into sports. It was my only outlet.

Unfortunately, I developed a distorted body image which became a severe eating disorder, I was anorexic and bulimic by the age of 17. My eating disorder almost took my life, at my lightest I weighed a mere 43kg, around 90 pounds, which at 5'9" meant I was emaciated. I was, however, the perfect weight for a model, my first career. I worked in Sydney, Milan, Paris, Switzerland and Germany for years until I could no longer survive my eating disorder. After living in Europe for two years, I came back to Australia, found a therapist and the beginnings of my emotional recovery started.

In the first nine months of my recovery, I quickly gained weight. I was super unhappy with the way my body looked, I was sedentary, smoking cigarettes, and I felt lost. I knew going on a diet was not the answer. In 1985 I went to a gym and took an aerobics class. I wish I could say I enjoyed it, but I didn't! The mirrors showed me a body I was ashamed of, and I couldn't keep up with the fast pace of the class. The instructor was unfriendly, I was filled with jealousy at how everyone looked good, and my body image was severely distorted. It was not the place for me. I then found a 50-meter outdoor pool located a 40-minute walk from where I lived, and this marked the start of my physical recovery process, a return to fitness. I had come back to my roots and rediscovered my love of swimming!

Daily, I walked to the pool, swam my laps, and walked home feeling better. I got hooked on that feeling. After a few months I quit smoking, started running to the pool and got a bicycle to commute around Sydney. I quickly lost the extra weight and became healthy and fit for the first time in years. After a wonderful season at the pool when winter came and the pool closed, at the suggestion of a friend I went to the gym for an aerobics class. This time I loved it! From my first class I was hooked!

After losing the extra weight I felt emotionally strong enough to go back to modeling but was fired from a job for being too big! Too big at a size four! Too big when I was fit and healthy for the first time in my career! Too big! This was clearly not the career for me. I couldn't conceive of representing women in that way, so I quit. I went into the modeling agency and told them I would rather "clean toilets for a living than be a model." I was done and had no idea what I would do!

My favorite instructor at the gym suggested I take a course on how to become a fitness leader, then called ACHPER, and in 1986 I became a certified fitness leader. After taking a course, passing an exam and doing 40-hours of supervised work, I got registered. I was so excited by the possibilities! Physical fitness had changed my life and not just in how I looked. It was more in how I felt about myself. It lifted my mood, it energized me, it spoke to my soul! Now I had the opportunity to share that!

I've never looked back at the modeling world. In fitness I found my life's mission: to make a difference! In 1990 I came to Los Angeles to take the IDEA Foundation Aerobics Instructor Certification (now called ACE). I wanted to teach continuing education to instructors and knew I had to continue my own education if I was to make that dream a reality. I was soon hired to teach classes at Voight Fitness and Dance Studios in West Hollywood. I quickly developed a celebrity following and was asked to audition for a part as an instructor leading a workout in a fitness video with Cher.

In 1991 I shot and led the fitness video, "Cher Fitness, A New Attitude," and my career shot into the media focus. I was training Cher and a host of other celebrities. I became the answer to a question on Jeopardy, and I was very much in the spotlight. While touring with Cher during her Love Hurts World Tour, I once again relapsed into bulimia and anorexia. The constant travel, being away from my support system and the media focus was too much. My focus had also changed. It was, once again, all about how I looked and being a certain size. I was lost.

For the next several years I struggled, moving in and out of severe depression, food, alcohol and drug abuse. I was in a very dark place. The only light, the only thing that kept me going, was teaching classes and training clients. I saw that I could be helpful, that I could make a difference and that kept me surviving. Over all the ups and downs the one constant, the number one comfort, was how I felt once I was working out. I wanted to share that. I wanted to pass that on, and I had the knowledge, experience and passion to do it.

In 1999 I was diagnosed with bipolar disorder and under the guidance of a capable, compassionate doctor, put on medication. It saved my life. Without a doubt I had relied on exercise to "fix" me, but no amount of exercise was enough, and once I was medicated and finding balance, my life's intention came into focus yet again. Teaching classes, training clients gave me a true sense of purpose. Sharing my love of fitness made me feel alive. It still does!

During the mid 90's I was introduced to the sport of cycling. Cycling was like a missing piece of a puzzle that I had long lost and suddenly found. I was no longer bulimic or anorexic, but my body image was still distorted and my relationship with food was like a cold war. I knew I had to eat, but I didn't enjoy it. I was doing everything I could to control my eating but there was little enjoyment, and I still didn't really like myself.

Cycling forced me to eat, it forced me to fuel myself, and it wasn't about the way I looked. There was no focus on my appearance. If I wanted to perform well, I had to eat. Period! This missing piece fell into place, I was finally able to freely eat to nourish my body so I could perform and do what I loved. The sport helped me to fully recover from my eating disorder and be able to move forward in my life in a meaningful way.

Over the years there have been many defining moments that have driven my love of fitness. The first came when I re-discovered swimming and found a love of fitness in my 20's. The second came at the beginning of my career in Australia, when a young man who had been living with obesity started taking my class. After a year or so of participating in my sessions he lost over 250 pounds and was now a healthy weight for the first time in his life. He came to me and told me that it was my influence, my classes, that had been the catalyst for his transformation. The third was when I discovered the sport of cycling, and I developed a healthy relationship with food and my body.

Since then, my focus in fitness has led me to launch my own on-demand video platform. After I did the enormously popular fitness video with Cher, I was invited to film my own series of videos with CBS/Fox. These workouts and the informercial that went with them sold hundreds of thousands of VHS tapes and I went on to film for many different companies with a wide variety of workouts, from Step, Kickboxing, Rebounder, strength and conditioning and Body Bar. I have released videos in the UK, Australia and I even filmed two ski conditioning videos in Italy with Olympic Gold Medalist Alberto Tomba. In more recent years my filming has been for American Specialty Health, Silver and Fit and Active and Fit.

Until recently I had never filmed for myself, for my own brand and philosophy, now with my on-demand platform I have an exciting opportunity to deliver fitness programs for people in all walks of life who need safe, effective, fun and convenient training options. While I'm no longer in my 20's, 30's, 40's or 50's, I know that my wisdom, forty years of experience, extensive knowledge and passion can guide people to find their own health and fitness awakening. Just like Elaine LaLanne, I know that it's never too late to inspire and motive.

I first met Elaine several years ago, her energy, her passion and her drive inspired me beyond words. Elaine has that fire inside that I recognize and identify with myself. Her legacy paves the way for fitness professionals like me. Elaine proves that age is just a number, that it's never too late to follow your heart. Jack LaLanne was the perfect example of ageless aging and it's what I aspire to. Jack and Elaine both exemplify what a healthy lifestyle and fitness can do.

The LaLanne legacy of health and fitness is a torch that must be carried on, and I feel I have a responsibility to carry that message. Anyone, no matter who you are, can improve the quality of your life by gaining and maintaining a healthier lifestyle through exercise, nutrition and a positive outlook. It doesn't require an expensive gym membership, a complicated routine or fancy equipment. All it takes is a little willingness to get started.

Early in my journey I was motivated to fitness because I wanted to lose weight. Once I started moving and exercising, I realized that it made me feel better, it gave me energy, helped me sleep better and brightened my mood. Motivation comes and goes; I learned that discipline was more important. That with discipline I show up and get it done. With discipline, I create a habit and with a habit I don't need willpower or motivation. That is what turned my life around, and it can do that for yours too.

I went the wrong way and found my way back. On my way back to health and fitness I found something beautiful. The journey became the destination and, as a result, I discovered my life purpose. Your life purpose may have nothing to do with health or fitness, but I can guarantee you this, your life will transform beyond your imagination if you just get started. What are you waiting for?

Keli Roberts

Keli Roberts has been recognized for many prestigious awards in the fitness industry. In 2003, she was named the IDEA International Fitness Instructor of the year. In 2011, Keli was awarded the Best Female Presenter for Empower! Conventions and in 2022 she received the Equinox Group Fitness Lifetime Achievement Award. In 2007 she was inducted into the National Fitness Hall of Fame. Keli is an American College of Sports Medicine Exercise Physiologist and holds certifications through American Council on Exercise as a Group Fitness Instructor, Health Coach, Certified Personal Trainer and Senior Exercise Specialist. Additionally, Keli is a certified Personal trainer through Functional Aging Institute, National Academy of Sports Medicine Corrective Exercise Specialist and International Sports Sciences Association Brain Trainer and Exercise Recovery Specialist.

Chapter 15

Resilience Rewritten:
Faith, Fitness, and the Ripple Effect

By Janelle Trujillo

Do you remember the first time weight and size became part of your consciousness?

I was about twelve years old. It was the early '90s—there was no social media yet, but magazines, commercials, and TV shows were everywhere, quietly planting seeds. At first it was just curiosity, a flicker of attention. By around fifteen, it started to sink deeper, twisting into something heavier.

By sixteen, I was secretly saving money to buy the latest issue of SHAPE magazine or any cover that promised "10 pounds gone in a week." Before I turned seventeen, I had a full-blown eating disorder. I remember standing in front of the mirror and truly hating the girl staring back at me. I was a competitive athlete and a straight-A student, yet I was convinced my value was tied to my external image, specifically my weight and size.

Body dysmorphia and depression trapped me in a cycle of relentless negative thoughts, scrutinizing every inch of myself, believing a smaller frame would finally earn me acceptance, not so much from others, but for myself. The voices grew louder until, at seventeen, they nearly ended my life in a suicide attempt.

In the hospital, surrounded by family, friends, and prayers, something shifted. Their love reminded me that my worth was not tied to my appearance or accomplishments. That moment became my turning point, my first conscious choice to reject the lie that my body defined me. I began to see it as a vessel for strength and purpose, not shame or an impossible standard. One small choice to accept love and see my identity as a child of God.

After high school, I enrolled in a community college course called "How to Teach Group Fitness," hoping to build a healthier relationship with exercise. On the first day, I walked in early and saw a whiteboard with a simple circle and four arrows pointing to Physical, Mental, Emotional, and Spiritual, with "WELLNESS" written in the center. That diagram lit something inside me. I realized my purpose was not to chase an idealized image or external validation, but to help others find balance across every dimension of health.

I began choosing differently each day: picking up a journal to process my feelings, turning to prayer to restore my faith, and moving my body with kindness instead of criticism. Those small but consistent choices reshaped fitness for me, from a source of shame into a pathway to mental clarity, emotional grounding, and spiritual renewal.

That shift propelled me into my first professional role in wellness: teaching group fitness classes. I stood in front of rooms full of hopeful faces and witnessed something beautiful, people letting go of appearance-driven goals and embracing wellness rooted in real strength, vibrant health, and deep vitality. They walked out taller, moved with confidence and ease, and carried a contagious quiet joy into their everyday lives.

Hungry to understand the body I was now helping others honor, I pursued and earned my degree in Kinesiology. The deeper I delved in my knowledge, the more I marveled at the intricate design and sheer beauty of the human body, and the undeniable truth that mind, body, and spirit are not separate, but one interconnected whole. When one thrives, the others follow; when one suffers, the others feel it too. That profound realization became the heart of my coaching: a truly holistic approach that addresses every dimension of health. From those first classes to today, I've seen again and again that our daily choices, from our mindsets, to moving our bodies, to nourishment, to grow, don't just change us. They send out ripples of resilience, confidence, and life that touch far more people than we will ever know.

The journey continued, but the struggles with self-worth did not simply vanish. For years I carried those deep wounds, and they led me into an unhealthy marriage, followed by a long separation and, eventually, divorce. Healing was slow and nonlinear. Yet in time, I met an extraordinary man, now my husband. He showed me what unconditional love and true acceptance feel like. He helped remind me of my gifts and that they had nothing to do with my external looks but the purpose God created me for.

Through this relationship, I discovered a truth that changed everything, and I want you to hold it close: the people we choose to surround ourselves with have the power to shape our becoming. They can either lift us into healing, hope, and wholeness, or hold us back in old pain. But here is the glorious part, we also get to choose to be that light for someone else. The choices we make in our relationships, in who we allow close and who we become for others.

Having chosen a partner who reminded me daily of the purpose God had placed in me, I was better equipped to see life's challenges as opportunities rather than obstacles.

The perfect example came in March 2020. My husband and I moved from New Mexico to downtown Seattle just as the pandemic forced health clubs across the country to close. We arrived in a city transformed into a ghost town: streets that once pulsed with commuters, tourists, and the hum of coffee shops were now deserted, storefronts dark, sidewalks empty except for the occasional masked figure hurrying past. There was nowhere to gather, only the heavy silence of lockdown and a constant, low hum of fear about an invisible threat.

In the midst of that compounded stress, a new city, no familiar routines, the weight of global uncertainty pressing in, I did what had always steadied me. I leaned into the practices that kept me anchored: prayer, movement, and service. Within days, I pivoted to daily online workouts. I set up a simple corner in our apartment with a yoga mat, resistance bands, a few free weights and my phone propped on a stack of books. Every morning at 7 a.m., I went live on Instagram and Facebook offering free, full-body sessions that blended strength, mobility, and encouragement. I was genuinely excited, eager to serve my community at a moment when everyone suddenly had more time than ever and, I believed, a deeper need for something grounding and hopeful.

Yet only fifteen of my 1,600 followers showed up consistently.

That low turnout became my lightbulb moment. Time was never the real barrier to health. We all had extra hours, but most people coped with unprecedented stress through whatever habits were already wired into them—unconscious patterns built for quick relief. Uber Eats and Netflix became two of the fastest-growing companies of that era for a reason. People weren't choosing movement or nourishing food because those choices weren't yet their automatic response to stress.

If I truly wanted to help, I had to go deeper than offering workouts, I had to teach people how to build sustainable habits that supported their health, even under pressure. That realization propelled me into an immersive study of the science and psychology of habit formation, exploring how small, intentional actions could rewire stress responses and create lasting change.

And the first place I applied this habit reshaping was in our own home, the perfect real-time testing ground. As my husband stepped into a managing partner role at a new firm amid deep economic chaos, and I grappled with the move, we both turned to the same small habits I was studying: earlier bedtimes for restorative sleep, nourishing meals cooked together when we could, morning movement side by side or solo, brief meditations, and moments of prayer throughout the day. Simple, consistent acts that asked little yet transformed much giving me steady focus and reframed perspective, him calmer leadership and sharper clarity, and us a shared peace that proved the power of those choices under real pressure.

Those experiences crystallized my calling: to bring habit-based transformation to high-achieving executives and business owners who face constant pressure. I now coach other leaders, using a proven framework that integrates fitness, nutrition, and mindfulness without demanding more time, just smarter, sustainable habits. One client shared that our work helped her sleep deeply for the first time in years and lead with greater empathy, ultimately shifting her entire company culture. The choices we make for our own wellness do not stop with us; they ripple into teams, families, and organizations.

Looking back, it astonishes me how far God has brought me, from a broken teenager who believed she had no purpose and no worth, to a woman fully alive in the calling He placed on my life, guiding leaders toward the same freedom and strength I once thought impossible.

To everyone reading this: wherever you are right now, whether you're standing in front of a mirror hearing the same harsh voices I once did, carrying wounds that still ache, or simply feeling like your story has already written its ending, know this: you are not done yet. Your journey is still unfolding, and the most powerful chapters are often the ones that come after the hardest battles.

Every struggle you face is forging strength in you, and not just for your own healing, but so you can one day extend a hand to someone walking the same dark path and say, "I've been there, and there is a way through." Your pain is becoming your purpose.

True strength rises from faith, courage, and the quiet power of small, intentional choices—especially the choice to speak love to yourself when the old voices try to return. You don't have to be perfect; you only have to be willing to keep growing, to keep choosing light over darkness, hope over despair. A morning workout, a moment of prayer, a kind word offered to someone else. These are not small things, they are acts of defiance against defeat, declarations that you are still becoming.

And every one of those choices, even the unseen ones inside your mind and heart, sends out a ripple effect far beyond yourself, touching lives, shifting atmospheres, and rewriting stories you may never fully see. You are not finished. You are being made new, and the world needs the resilient, radiant version of you that is still emerging.

The beautiful mystery of this journey is that just when we begin to grasp how far our choices can reach, God often sends someone whose life has already been sending those same ripples for decades. Their example becomes a living invitation to keep going, to keep choosing growth, and to trust that our becoming is never wasted. For me, that living invitation arrived in the form of Elaine LaLanne, a woman whose century of joyful, faithful living embodies everything I now teach.

Elaine's infectious enthusiasm has built communities rooted in health and joy. Yet she is far more than a fitness enthusiast. She is a profound inspiration to women everywhere. Known as the "First Lady of Fitness," Elaine was a true trailblazer in a male-dominated industry, co-hosting shows, producing groundbreaking content, and helping build a fitness empire as Jack LaLanne's devoted wife and indispensable partner for over fifty-one years. A loving mother, accomplished businesswoman who continues to lead BeFit Enterprises. She exemplifies the strength of balancing family, partnership, career, and personal vitality with grace.

When I had the pleasure of meeting and getting to know this amazing woman, I asked her what the most important thing for health and longevity is (besides exercise and nutrition). She answered without hesitation: "Mindset." She emphasized maintaining a positive outlook and never using age as an excuse to slow down or stop growing. At one hundred years old, Elaine truly embodies this truth, prioritizing longevity through an unshakable belief in continuous growth over perfection.

Elaine's words on mindset mirror my own transformation—from a young woman trapped in negative self-talk to the resilient coach I am today who chooses positivity, growth, and inner strength every day. Her insight ties it all together: true wellness and longevity begin in the mind. And the choices we make there—the thoughts we nurture, the beliefs we reinforce—send out the widest ripples of all.

Elaine's legacy reminds us that fitness is a celebration of life, purpose, and community. Let's honor her by taking one brave step, and one positive thought, toward wellness, knowing each choice sends out a ripple effect of resilience, joy, and transformation far beyond ourselves.

Janelle Trujillo

As a young adult, the scales of this world – success, appearance, approval – measured Janelle's worth. Desperate for validation, she spiraled into dangerous cycles of striving for perfection. An honor student, she chased the world's acceptance, believing a size 0 and less than 100 pounds would finally make her enough. Even at her thinnest, shame consumed her. Weight fluctuations triggered self-hatred; she felt she would never be enough. The darkness led to depression's lowest point – a suicide attempt that, by the grace of God, she survived.

That turning point became her calling. Janelle vowed to help others discover what she learned the hard way: true health and happiness isn't your jeans size or a competition trophy. It's the daily habits that heal the mind, strengthen the body, restore the spirit, and silence the inner critic for good.

From turning five failing personal-training departments into profit engines to building Janelle4Health into a six-figure online coaching system, Janelle has coached hundreds to sustainable transformation. Today, she works exclusively with CEOs and executives, delivering signature nine-month programs that integrate sleep mastery, strategic nutrition, movement that restores rather than punishes, and mindset rituals rooted in faith and gratitude.

Her message is simple yet revolutionary: stop chasing perfection. Start building habits that let you thrive – at work, at home, and in the quiet moments when only you and God know the victory. It is never too late to rewrite your story and live strong, healthy, and free – not just for a season, but for a lifetime.

Connect with Janelle:

Instagram: @Janelle4health
Facebook & LinkedIn: Janelle Trujillo

Chapter 16

Believe. Adapt. Achieve.

By Dolly Stokes

My name is Jane, but throughout my life, I have been known as Dolly. This family nickname was given to me by my father, inspired by the popular Louie Armstrong song from 1964, "Hello, Dolly!" The name has stuck with me ever since and has become a cherished part of my identity.

I am the sixth of seven children, with five brothers and one sister. Growing up during the 1960s and 1970s shaped my experiences in unique ways. Back then, your friends were usually the kids who lived nearby, and for me, that meant spending most of my time outside playing a variety of sports and playing in the woods in our backyard with my brothers. This love of being outdoors and moving became the foundation for my lifelong career in health and fitness.

However, there was a brief period during my freshman year of college where a combination of unhealthy habits resulted in a significant weight gain – nearly 50 pounds, which was far more than the typical "freshman 15."

Defining Moments on My Journey

When I was 19, I decided to pursue a career in the legal field. My first job was as a receptionist for a law firm. This began my 20-year career as a legal assistant and paralegal.

One day, as Scott, one of the senior partners of the firm entered the office, he stopped at my desk. He told me that he and his wife would like me to join them for aerobics at the YMCA that was about a block from the office. He basically said, "You are smart and have a good work ethic, but you need to lose some weight. We think aerobics would help. If you enjoy it, we will pay for your membership." I was embarrassed that he pointed out the obvious – that I was overweight so I thanked him and told him I would think about it.

A few days later, my Daddy said basically the same thing to me about needing to lose some weight. It was at this point that I said to myself, "I don't need to hear this from a third person." So, I accepted Scott's offer to join him and his wife for aerobics.

After that first class, I was hooked! That class changed my life. This led to healthy nutritional habits and regularly scheduled exercise which included aerobics, weight training and long-distance cycling.

While working full-time as a paralegal, when I was 22, I began working part-time in the fitness field as a personal trainer and teaching fitness classes. Through the years, I developed my own style of fitness programs that blended strength, mobility, and holistic wellness. In 2002, I began working for FiTOUR as a ProTrainer.

In 2004, I had a paradigm shift that allowed me to step away from my career in the legal field and commit to full-time fitness training. A spiritual gifts course at church helped me align my strengths – leadership, teaching, and encouragement – with my calling. Completing this class bolstered my confidence and allowed me to leave my secure job and start DollyBFitness Consulting which is now operating as Stokes-Method. In 2007, FiTOUR promoted me to the role of Director of Education where I served for 10 years. I continue to work for FiTOUR as part of the research and development team.

Connection to Elaine LaLanne's Legacy

I met Elaine LaLanne at the 2017 IDEA World Fitness Convention while registering with my husband, Jeff. Recognizing her immediately, I introduced myself and my husband. She was energetic and friendly, preferring to be called "LaLa" instead of Mrs. LaLanne. Rather than talking about herself, she wanted to learn about us and our roles in fitness. She kindly took the time to take a picture with me, insisting that we both show off our "guns". Meeting LaLa was one of the highlights of the convention that year.

LaLa reminds me of my grandmother Mae, who greatly influenced me. Like LaLa, Mae had a strong faith, valued health, exercised regularly, and maintained a classic sense of style.

The examples of Mae and LaLa inspire me to stay active, positive and purposeful as I age.

My Message of Empowerment

During the spring of 2010, I experienced impaired coordination in my left leg and arm, persistent sensations of cold despite hot weather, difficulty sensing my left limbs, and cognitive issues such as memory recall and word finding problems.

My symptoms progressively worsened and by the fall of 2011, I was diagnosed with relapsing remitting multiple sclerosis with plaques located in areas of my brain that are responsible for cognition, mobility and speech.

At the age of 47, I had achieved peak physical fitness, DollyBFitness was thriving, and my position with FiTOUR was progressing success-fully

My neurologist told me that my days of high-intensity workouts that included body building, running half marathons and competing in triathlons were over – that I could expect to be in a wheelchair by the time I was 60. But a second opinion provided hope and allowed me to see that life as I knew it was not over. In fact, the diagnosis would take me down a different path.

With the loving support of my husband, I learned not to allow MS to define me. That all I needed to do was to believe in myself, adapt to situations as they arise, and achieve the optimal that I can each day. This has inspired my motto "Believe. Adapt. Achieve".

While I no longer participate in events like body building shows, triathlons and half-marathons, I continue to do all the fitness activities that I enjoyed before my diagnosis. I do weight room workouts, perform daily cardio through walking, running and cycling, practice Pilates and yoga, and perform self-myofascial release to keep my fitness and func-tional levels high.

Closing Thoughts & Legacy Statement

Looking back, I can see that my strong faith in God has been most in-strumental in my carving a path to a productive and happy life.

Whether trusting in God to be with me when I was told at the age of 28 that I would most likely never become pregnant to trusting that He would provide when I was a single mom working hard to get a new business off the ground to sending me a loving and caring husband who has been a steady bulwark through all of life's ups and downs.

When I first started my journey as a fitness pro so many years ago, I had goals to be a presenter and educator and to have my own business. All paths have led me to accomplish all my career goals and to a life that is filled with love and happiness.

I view my diagnosis of MS as a blessing. It allowed me to slow down and to focus on my health, rather than my fitness and appearance. This slowing down allowed me to be a better wife, mother, and friend. It also helped me to develop compassion for others who suffer from debilitating conditions.

When I reflect on the legacy I hope to pass down, it is to be remembered as a strong, compassionate woman who believed in herself, adapted to situations, and achieved her dreams.

Dolly Stokes

A powerhouse of information and enthusiasm, Dolly Stokes is a leader in fitness education. Drawing on her more than 35 years of experience as a fitness pro, Dolly has researched and authored many of FiTOUR's top-selling education courses including Myofascial Release, Boot Camp, and Active Aging courses.

She has been a certified group fitness instructor since 1989 and a certified personal trainer since 1992. She is a certified massage therapist; and holds over 30 fitness specialty certifications including ACSM Certified Inclusive Fitness Trainer, NASM Senior Fitness Specialist, Balanced Body Reformer Specialist, and FAI Functional Aging Specialist and Stroke Recovery Specialist. She presented her signature H.E.A.T. (High Energy Aquatics Training) aqua bootcamp at the 2010 IDEA World and was a plenary speaker at PCORI 2019 in Washington, DC.

She has traveled throughout the US and internationally training hundreds of fitness professionals. From 2015 to 2020, Dolly served on a research team through the University of Alabama Birmingham/Lakeshore Rehabilitation Collaborative to assist in designing an exercise intervention for people with multiple_sclerosis (MS). Her expertise in yoga and Pilates helped develop a program for four different functional levels of MS, and two additional levels for people with MS who also had osteoporosis.

Dolly and her husband, Jeff, own the StokesMethod Studio in Fairhope, Alabama. Their training programs are centered around Pilates reformer, myofascial release, corrective exercise and functional training.

When not training, Dolly and Jeff enjoy spending time on the water and at the beach with their family and four grandchildren.

www.stokesmethod.com
Instagram: @stokesmethod
Facebook: @stokesmethod
YouTube: @stokesmethod1234

Chapter 17

Three Hearts, One Beat

By Stephanie Muir

What do you say to the girl who is staring off into the dark, getting lost in the void?

What do you say to the girl who has not only lost her way but lost herself along the way?

What do you say to the girl who doesn't recognize her reflection in the mirror?

I used to be the girl with a smile on her face, a thirst for adventure, and who believed in silver linings. I had plans, goals, and checklists. Whether it was becoming a Registered Nurse, training for and running marathons, or DIY projects, I followed the steps and made things happen. I was independent and in control of my life. Or so I thought.

On June 30, 2011, I found myself helpless, lying in a hospital bed, unable to stop those unwanted contractions. Due to the medication I was on, I was unable to change position without someone else's help. I was dependent on others and without a plan. I found all I could do was pray and hope that God heard me and that the doctor's interventions would work. Despite the most raw and earnest prayers I have ever prayed, they went seemingly unanswered.

My husband and I had been married for about five years when we decided it was time to start a family. That did not come easy for us. Month after month turned into year after year of our dreams of having a baby being denied. During that struggle with infertility, it caused my husband and me to pause and reflect on why we wanted children. Did we only want to have a baby, or did we have a deep desire to raise a child? Would we be okay if the dream of parenthood never came to fruition? While we desperately wanted to have a baby, we wanted the responsibility and honor of raising a child even more.

With the help of a fertility doctor, I was able to become pregnant with our first daughter. She was a dream come true, my living proof that God answers prayers. Two years later, we were pleasantly surprised to learn I was pregnant again. We were told by our fertility doctor that we would not be able to get pregnant without the help of modern medicine, and yet, the second pregnancy came naturally. That pregnancy surprised us again when we learned I was pregnant with identical twins. I thanked and praised God for this miracle. We spent a few weeks in shock as the realization of having three kids, two years of age and under, set in. I was mentally preparing myself to be completely immersed in diapers, bottles, finger foods, and having my days ruled by nap schedules. I also worried about our oldest daughter and the shadow the attention of identical twins would cast on her. Those worries and concerns were sprinkled in between the vast excitement and gratitude I felt in even being pregnant again, and with two babies! I did not take it for granted.

I was excited to have the weight of them in each of my arms, for those middle-of-the-night feeds when it feels like the rest of the world has melted away, and to see my oldest daughter interact with her two younger sisters. There were so many things I wondered. Would my twins have that twin speak you hear about sometimes with other twins? Would they be alike in personality or be so distinctly different that one would find it hard to believe that they looked exactly alike, even while looking at them? Would they want to dress alike, or separate themselves from the other as much as possible? Would they have the same friends, or would they orbit in different social circles? Would they be so close together that their older sister would feel like they were always out of her reach, or would one twin be closer to her older sister than her own twin? Would they all get along, or would they constantly be annoyed with each other? I sketched with black ink what I thought my life and theirs would be. I was anxiously waiting to see how they would color their world.

I was busy planning and preparing and dreaming for these two new lives, blissfully and innocently moving forward. Then, my husband and I were blindsided at a scheduled ultrasound appointment when we learned something was terribly wrong. I was diagnosed with Twin-to-Twin Transfusion Syndrome. It is a condition that occurs when identical twins share a placenta, and there is an unequal distribution of blood flow. One twin is receiving too much blood, while the other twin is not receiving enough. It is dangerous and possibly deadly for both.

I underwent surgery, and afterwards, everything was looking better than expected. I still had a long road ahead, but we were filled with hope. As my husband and I were preparing to go to sleep for the night, a sharp, shooting pain came out of nowhere. I was in labor, and it was too soon. The rest of the night was spent trying medical intervention after medical intervention to stop the labor. I spent the rest of the night pleading with God.

As the day dawned, I knew the outcome was bleak.

Twelve and a half hours after labor began, I gave birth to Emmerson Claire. She was a pound, and she had her older sister's eyes and lips. When the doctor raised her up after delivery for us to look at her, she moved her arm as if in a wave, as if to say hello. She was placed on my chest, and my husband held one of her hands, marveling at her tiny fingernails. He told her that the nail cutting was his job and that hers already needed a trim. We soaked her up. We tried to tell her how much we loved her and how much we were looking forward to her joining our family. As she lay in my arms, with her dad holding one of her hands, we sang *Jesus Loves Me* to her as her heart stopped beating.

Even though my heart had been shattered, holding her as she passed from this life into the arms of her King has been one of the greatest honors of my life. There was so much peace and love in that room when she died, and I hope she felt every ounce of it. I hope all that little girl felt was love.

Twin B was still alive after her sister passed away. She was looking strong, so they increased the medications that stop labor. The plan was to keep me in the hospital for a few more weeks, getting me and Twin B to a place where she stood a better chance of survival outside of the womb. I was in a state I had never been in before. I was filled with grief over the death of one of my babies while simultaneously filled with hope that another one would make it. How can someone be expected to dance between the two? From somewhere in the depths, I was wondering how I would look at this baby every day and not see the one who was missing.

For five hours, everything looked good, and then the other shoe dropped. Twin B's heart had stopped beating. I remember looking at the monitor, waiting for my heart to stop as well. Or maybe I was wishing for it, I am not sure. How can one of the most joyous times in life be filled with shrapnel from a shattered heart?

The medications to stop labor were discontinued, and it was only after they were stopped that my body finally responded to them. After it no longer mattered, the contractions stopped. I was then given medications to induce labor. While we waited for those medications to start doing their job, I started losing blood.

We waited and waited, but the medications were failing to do what they were supposed to do, and I was still bleeding. I had to sign a consent form for a Cesarean Section. If I did not deliver Twin B by a decided-upon time, I would have to go in for surgery. The medications to induce labor started working, and I was able to deliver Twin B before surgery was warranted. After the delivery of Twin B, I signed a consent form for a hysterectomy because my body refused to let go of the placenta. The hysterectomy would occur if I didn't deliver the placenta within thirty minutes. I was still losing a lot of blood, so I signed a consent form for a blood transfusion. With moments to spare, I was spared a hysterectomy.

Twelve and a half hours after Emmerson was born, Vivienne Catherine was placed in my arms. She was the twin who was not getting enough blood flow, so she was a little smaller than her sister. Other than her smaller size, she looked just like Emmerson, while both of them looked like their older sister.

What do you do with all of those hopes and dreams for a future that is no longer possible?

I left the hospital the next day, a shell of who I had been. Though my heart had not been one of the ones that had stopped, something in me had died. I had stopped seeing in color. I wanted to go back in time, to rewrite what couldn't be undone. The months that followed were a blur of grief, disbelief, and survival.

When you are expecting a child, you hear that nothing comes close to the anticipation and arrival of that life. You would think that when your baby dies, you would be met with an understanding that losing a baby or pregnancy would be one of the worst things. However, we were met with a thousand *at-leasts* and the encouragement to just have another baby, as if another baby erases the memory and dream of the one who drifted away like a whisper. Being told to have another baby isn't a salve to the bleeding wound. It is not just a moment in time that is grieved. It's grieving the first words and first steps, the first day of kindergarten and a first love. It's kissing away the hurt from scraped knees that will never be and shopping for prom dresses that will never be worn. It's all the missed birthdays that never got a flame to burn, that never got to see the flame hushed by excited breath. It's the white gown, veil, and flowers, and not being able to give them away on their wedding day. It's not that the one death is the final act. Instead, it is that the one death is the precursor to a million more. It's a loss that gives birth to more loss. For those of us who had to utter an all-too-soon goodbye, we are left with hopes and dreams that have nowhere to go.

Fortunately, I did not need to have a hysterectomy, but that didn't mean I wanted to have another baby. I was terrified of getting pregnant again and risking losing again. So, I decided we were done having children. However, eight months after I had the twins, I learned I was pregnant. I was an anxious ball of nerves during that pregnancy. I refused to prepare for a life where we brought a baby home. I prepared for the heaviness of empty arms and silence, rather than the cries of life. With almost three months left in my pregnancy, I went into preterm labor causing all those anxieties and fears to grip me tighter. I went into overdrive preparing for the worst. When our son entered our world, five weeks early, he filled the sun-drenched room with his wails, declaring that he was here. Those fears had grabbed hold so tightly that I couldn't hear that reassuring sound. Through sobs rising from the black depths, I kept asking if he was alive. And then, suddenly, his pink, screaming body reached me lifting me out of fear's crushing grip. My infant son helped me see in color again.

However, even though life was moving forward, I was not. I smiled, worked and mothered, but I was only merely surviving. I still had all those hopes and dreams hanging with nowhere to go.

A few years later, the sun reached through the window and lay itself lazily across the floor as I was putting fresh sheets on my bed. There was something about the fresh scent of linen, intertwined with the golden light, that sparked a memory of a dream. That flash of memory stopped me mid-motion. For the first time, I saw how far grief had carried me away from the girl I once knew and the mom I had wanted to be. I was only enduring life, not living it.

What do you say to the girl who got lost in the void, to the girl who lost herself along the way? I had made a promise to my twins that I would live for them, but if I couldn't live life fully, how could I honor that promise? And not only was I failing to honor my twins, but I was also failing at being present for my two living children. So, I asked myself what made me feel alive. The answer came easily: movement, adventure, and the open world. The re-realization of what set my soul on fire sparked a crazy dream. In 2019, we sold our home and most of our belongings. Along with my husband, our two children, and our dog, we moved into a fifth wheel and spent the next three and a half years traveling across the United States.

It was a drastic and bold decision that garnered both praise and criticism. The criticism didn't bother us because we knew some hard truths about life that our critics didn't quite understand. While some viewed it as a bold choice, we knew it was necessary. We had learned painfully that life is fragile and can be cut way too short. Emmerson and Vivienne's deaths taught us that time is a thief, and children don't keep.

That drastic step was one of the best decisions we have ever made. When you stand before your child's grave, the last thread of innocence is lost. I am fearful of burying another child, but instead of letting that fear hold me back and keep my world small, I choose to live audaciously. I like to think grief taught me to cherish the sweet moments amid the bitterness. It makes me pause and memorize the cadence of my children's laughter so I can replay it in my mind. Or how I branded the feel of their little hands in mine, so when they stopped reaching for me, I could still feel the warmth of their touch. I became a mom who said yes more than no, knowing that in the end, all we get to carry with us are the memories we make. With that one drastic step, we have memory banks full of adventure, conversations, and overcoming fears both big and small. Every mile, every sunset, every belly full of laughter was a way to honor Emmerson and Vivienne.

If it had not been for Emmerson and Vivienne, I wouldn't have dared to live so boldly. It is in that boldness that I see a kindred spirit in Elaine. She has been bold throughout her life, but she also knows loss and what it means to keep moving forward. With her undeniable strength and hunger for life, she carries the legacy of her husband, Jack, by continuing the work they began, just as I try to carry my twins' legacy by giving those hopes and dreams that once had nowhere to go, some place to call home.

I can look at someone like Elaine, and the word legacy seems to make sense. However, I have never given much thought to my own legacy. It feels big, too big for me to wrap my head around. Though, as a mother, I hope my children see more of the good in me than the bad and that, despite setbacks, I didn't stop dreaming. And despite the sharp edges of a shattered heart, knowing the cost of love, I never stopped loving them with a raw intensity. I hope they see a woman who took the broken pieces and decided to make something new.

Stephanie Muir

Stephanie Filicsky Muir is the author of the Amazon bestseller, *Hollows of the Oak: The Key*, which also won the Scriptor Publishing Group Pen to Prose Award for fiction. She loves to travel, collecting stamps in her passport book, and is always up for any outdoor adventure. She lives on five acres in a rural town in Indiana with her husband, two children, some chickens, and a dog. She is currently working on her second book and dreaming of adding more animals to the chaos.

Hollows of the Oak: The Key is available on Amazon.

You can find Stephanie on Instagram under muir_moments.

Chapter 18

Barriers into Bridges: Fitness as the Foundation of Resilience

By Carrie Armacost

"Strength doesn't come from what you can do. It comes from overcoming the things you once thought you couldn't."

– RIKKI ROGERS

Early Lessons in Motion

As the youngest of three children, my earliest lessons in resilience weren't learned in crisis, but in contrast. My sister was the scholar – sharp, steady, and effortlessly confident in classrooms. My brother was the athlete and budding entrepreneur – competitive, driven, already chasing success with the intensity of someone who knew exactly who he was becoming. And then there was me, the youngest, still finding my rhythm, quietly wondering where I fit among their shine.

I remember the sound of their laughter drifting down the hallway as they compared report cards or swapped stories of big wins. I often watched from the doorway – proud of them, yet hungry to be seen in my own light. Even then, I learned to listen first, to observe, to adapt. The air in our home buzzed with expectation, but I found my own calm in the spaces between – through curiosity, through people, through purpose.

Movement became the place where I could feel most like me-the most liberated. Before I had the words to describe myself, my body spoke for me. I ran, jumped, climbed, and tumbled my way toward confidence. On the field, the court, or even just the backyard grass beneath my feet, I didn't need perfect grades or polished speeches to feel worthy. I just needed motion. And in that motion, I felt free.

The rhythm of movement quickly became the rhythm of my life. Sports taught me that consistency builds strength, and that strength – both physical and emotional – would later become my anchor. Teams surrounded me with encouragement, teaching me that success is never a solo act. There is something sacred about a group chasing the same finish line – each person pushing, pulling, and elevating the other.

"To give anything less than your best is to sacrifice your gift."

– STEVE PREFONTAINE.

Sports became my first real teacher. From gripping a tee-ball bat at age four, to high-school basketball, field hockey, and golf, I learned discipline, structure, and what it meant to work toward a goal. College athletics sharpened those values even further. Coaches mentored me; captaining teams taught me to mentor others. Just as significant was the circle around me – teammates who trained hard, held each other accountable, and never let anyone fall behind. Looking back, those early seasons were building resilience inside me long before I knew how much I'd one day rely on it.

Those years planted something important in me – a drive not to outshine, but to belong. To compete by pushing *my own* limits. To contribute. To bring warmth, connection, and encouragement into every space I entered. That seed became the quiet foundation for everything that followed – from motherhood, to business, to the bridge I now stand on today.

A Leap of Faith – and My First Big Lesson in Uncertainty

At twenty-seven, I stepped off the predictable path and into the unknown. I didn't realize then that sometimes strength asks you to start over long before you feel ready. After several miscarriages – each one carrying its own quiet ache of doubt and fear – I finally found myself seven and a half months pregnant, preparing to leave a career I loved, pack up a life I understood, and move clear across the country.

The day we arrived, the air felt heavy with both anticipation and uncertainty. Our temporary home – a tiny 800-square-foot apartment – echoed with unfamiliar quiet. I can still hear the low hum of the refrigerator breaking the stillness, a small reminder that life was continuing even as everything felt suspended.

Movers clanged up two flights of stairs, maneuvering boxes through narrow doorways, trying to make oversized furniture fit into modest rooms. What didn't fit went into the garage, stacked like a holding zone for the pieces of our life that hadn't yet found a place. Our 90-pound Rottweiler paced endlessly, whining under her breath, unsettled by all the commotion and constant shifting. Even the small kitchen table had to double as my husband's office desk – another reminder that every part of our life now had to stretch, adjust, and adapt.

I was doing the same.

In that tiny space, I began preparing a new kind of home – a resting place that was barely a quarter of what we were used to – while stepping into a new role I wasn't sure I was ready for: mother, supportive wife, and the steady foundation beneath a husband whose career required constant travel in this unfamiliar corner of the Pacific Northwest.

It was time to pivot, and at a pace I didn't choose. Familiarity, family, and lifelong friends were now thousands of miles behind us in the Midwest. The support systems I had always counted on were suddenly gone, replaced with cardboard boxes, quiet evenings, and a landscape I didn't yet understand.

In time, it all began to settle into place. Our daughter was born, and we eventually built our new home, moved in, and found ourselves embraced by a warm community, new friends, and new routines. A little over two and a half years later, our son arrived, and our family began settling into its new rhythm.

Motherhood reshaped me. It softened my edges, taught patience, and redefined what success looked like. But even in those early days – rocking a newborn, navigating sleepless nights, building a home out of uncertainty – there remained a small, determined voice inside me whispering, *Don't forget who you are. There are lessons in all of this.*

Motherhood will always be the greatest and most rewarding achievement of my life.

Still, I promised myself that when the time was right, I'd step back into the career world – not as the woman I once was, but as someone wiser, deeper, and more grounded.

When Life Rewrote My Playbook

Approximately 15 years later, that promise was tested in ways I could never have imagined. After twenty years of marriage, I found myself at forty-two – divorced, bankrupt, and a single parent to two children. I had been out of the workforce for nearly two decades. The world had changed; I had changed. And yet, there was no time to pause and catch my breath.

The silence felt louder than any noise I'd ever known. I asked myself, *Where do I begin?*

No one trains for a crisis. We train for a goal – fitter, faster, stronger – but not for the days when our world collapses.

At first, I tried to outrun the pain. I filled every hour, pushed every boundary, clung to my identity as a "doer." Yet, beneath the hustle, fear whispered, *What if I can't do this? What if I'm not enough this time?*

The ground shifting under my feet. The darkest moment had arrived. There were days when I was barely holding it together for my children, even though on the inside I was falling apart. The squirrel of a brain inside me had me wrestling with terrifying fears: I was unsure of who I was, and the sudden collapse of my marriage and finances left me without direction. Depression hit me hard, pulling me into a darkness so deep that I even battled thoughts and plans of ending it all.

I was emotionally defeated, elephant tears rolling down my face, and crouched in the woods behind my house with a gun in my hands. Then the message arrived. I heard a voice through the chaos though no one was around. A flash of light from the photo of my children's faces illuminated in the depth of my darkness and I was reminded…that survival wasn't enough. I wanted to rise – not just for me, but for my children.

The very skills that had made me strong – discipline, drive, determination – also became my hiding places. It wasn't until I paused, truly paused, that I began to understand resilience isn't about never falling apart. It's about allowing yourself to break and then having the courage to rebuild differently.

That's when the deeper meaning of fitness revealed itself. It was no longer about physical goals. It became a tool for survival, a structure for healing, and a daily act of faith. Each workout wasn't about perfection – it was proof that I was still showing up, still fighting, still believing in my capacity to rise.

I didn't have answers, so I did the one thing I could control: I moved. Some days it was a short run, other days a simple lift. It wasn't about records. It was about choosing forward motion when everything else felt stuck. The fog didn't clear overnight, but each workout gave me proof that I was still here and still capable. Bit by bit, strength returned, then clarity. I began to see a path: if movement could pull me out of that valley, I could help others use it to climb their own.

Fear was constant – so was determination. Every day became an exercise in resourcefulness. I sold what I could, budgeted every dollar, and built a schedule around survival. But even in the chaos, there was this flicker of faith – an inner knowing that the life I was meant to live wasn't behind me. It was waiting to be rebuilt, one small choice at a time.

Fitness became my lifeline. It wasn't about abs or achievements; it was about control. When everything else felt unstable, my body was something I could still trust. Movement gave me a sense of progress when the rest of life stood still. I began training small groups in a garage, bringing together others who also needed more than a workout – they needed community. I leaned into the community that I knew and discovered what it took to write a business plan, sign a 5 year lease, became an entrepreneur and built a fitness studio. CareFit Personal Training Studio was born.

It wasn't glamorous. It was grassroots, gritty, and real. But it was *mine.*

Resilience in the Rain

"Resilience is not about avoiding the storm,
but learning to dance in the rain."

– VIVIAN GREENE

That became my mantra long before I realized it would also become my message.

My storm taught me that resilience is mostly about presence. It's about how you meet yourself when life stops following your plan. I stopped asking, "Why me?" and began asking, "What is this trying to teach me?" That shift changed everything. It opened my eyes to the work I needed to do – what needed to be strengthened, what needed to be softened, and what needed to be released. That is where clarity begins, and where calm slowly returns.

Those first few years post-divorce were marked by both tears and triumphs. There were days when I taught classes with a lump in my throat, smiling through the weight of unpaid bills or late-night worries. I learned to celebrate the smallest victories – the first steady paycheck, the laughter of clients who had become loyal friends, the moments when my children saw their mom refuse to give up.

On the hardest mornings, I'd lace up my shoes, step into my studio, and breathe through the ache. The air smelled faintly of rubber mats and quiet determination. Music hummed low, steady as a heartbeat. The first squat, the first push-up, the first drop of sweat – those were my prayers. I wasn't chasing numbers anymore; I was chasing peace.

CareFit wasn't born in a moment of success – it was born in survival. I didn't set out to build a business. I set out to build stability, structure, and hope. Each session, each conversation, each act of encouragement became a brick in the foundation of something bigger than I could see at the time.

Through fitness, I rediscovered who I was – not just a coach, not just a mother, but a woman capable of rebuilding from rubble. The studio walls that once echoed with uncertainty soon filled with music, laughter, and a new kind of strength. I realized I wasn't just training bodies – I was helping rebuild lives, starting with my own.

As I rebuilt, I also began letting go of the doubts that had settled in during those difficult years. Releasing that fear made room for trust to return, and that trust opened the door to the man who would become my husband. Brad's love helped restore the parts of me that had grown weary. He brought steadiness, joy, and a kind of partnership that lifted not only me, but my children as well. I could not be more grateful that my storm led me to him. Sometimes the darkest seasons really do hide the brightest gems.

From Breakdown to Breakthrough

There's something sacred about reaching your breaking point. It strips away the excess, leaving only what's true.

At first, I thought I had lost everything – marriage, security, identity. But as I began rebuilding, I saw that what I'd actually lost were the things that once defined me externally. What remained was *me* – the parts that had been quiet but strong all along.

Fitness gave me the framework. Coaching gave me the purpose. Faith gave me the courage to keep going.

As CareFit grew, so did my understanding of what true health means. It isn't measured by calories burned or miles logged; it's measured by connection – mind to body, body to spirit, person to person. My clients weren't just coming for workouts; they were coming to remember who they were, too.

That's how *Barriers into Bridges Coaching* was born. It was the natural evolution of everything I'd lived – turning pain into perspective, motion into meaning, survival into significance.

The Power of Community

When I look back at what has sustained me through every season, it's community. From childhood teams to client groups, I've always found strength in connection.

During my hardest years, it was often the clients sweating beside me who reminded me I wasn't alone. Together, we lifted more than weights – we lifted one another. We shared stories, struggles, and victories. Those bonds became a lifeline.

Community is where healing accelerates. When we witness someone else overcome, we begin to believe that we can, too. That's why I built CareFit not as a gym, but as a safe house – a place where growth is celebrated and vulnerability is welcomed.

If there's one thing my journey has taught me, it's that we heal faster when we heal together. The power of community is the heartbeat of every transformation I've witnessed.

I often think back to my early sports days – the high fives, the laughter, the shared exhaustion after a hard game. Those moments built more than skill; they built belonging. In adulthood, we often lose that. We isolate, believing our struggles are unique. But the truth is, every one of us has stood at the edge of something uncertain, wondering if we'll make it to the other side.

That's why I lead with connection. Whether it's a small-group session, a corporate workshop, or a coaching conversation, my purpose is to remind people that they're not alone. Together, we create momentum – momentum that turns barriers into bridges.

When people come to me, they're often exhausted from holding it all together. I see it in their shoulders, their eyes, their breath. The moment they realize they're safe to exhale, something powerful happens: the rebuilding begins. And once that spark reignites, there's no stopping the transformation that follows.

That's what this work is truly about – helping high achievers, especially those in transition, rediscover purpose, fulfillment, and a path back to themselves. Because the same strength that carries you through a workout can also carry you through a reinvention.

Legacy in Motion

If I've learned anything, it's that "Legacy isn't something you leave behind – it's something you live, every day, through the lives you touch."

My legacy is built on movement: the courage to keep going when life stands still, the decision to rebuild when everything falls apart, the willingness to share the journey so others know they're not alone.

Today, when I look at where I am- surrounded by a thriving community, a blended family, and a business that grew from brokenness-I feel both humbled and grateful. The path here wasn't straight, but it was meaningful. Every setback became a steppingstone. Every barrier became a bridge.

And that's what I hope to leave behind: not just a story of survival, but an invitation for others to find strength in their own storm – to build their bridge and cross into a life of purpose, peace, and possibility.

My experiences became the curriculum of my life. They shaped me into a coach who doesn't just preach resilience but *lives it*. Today, my greatest joy is helping others rediscover their own strength – one small, intentional choice at a time.

The Invitation

If you've ever wondered whether you can rebuild, the answer is YES. You can lift the weight of uncertainty, run toward possibility, and stand strong in your own comeback story. The key is to start-one mindful movement, one intentional breath, one courageous choice at a time.

Because resilience isn't something you find. It is something that you build.

And you build it brick by brick, moment by moment, you don't just survive-you thrive. You become living proof that barriers were never meant to stop you. They were meant to shape you into the bridge others will one day cross.

Carrie Armacost

Carrie Armacost is a certified trainer through ACE, Todd Durkin Impact Life Coach, Mindset Coach, Entrepreneur, motivational speaker, and author who pairs nearly 20 years of professional coaching experience with a powerful personal story of resilience – making her message both credible and relatable. She is the founder of **CareFit Personal Training Studio** and **Barriers into Bridges Coaching**, where she empowers high-achieving adults to discover fulfillment physically, emotionally, and spiritually.

Inspiring High Performers to Rebuild, Rise, and Thrive.

To connect with Carrie go to:

Website: www.carefitstudio.fitness.
IG: @CarrieArmacost
FB: @CarrieSchwartzArmacost

Chapter 19

A Little Girl's Dream, God's Bigger Plan

By Cherry Tapley

When I think about how I came to live a meaningful and purposeful life, it all goes back to my childhood. Like many little girls, I dreamed BIG, but my dream was simple. Every night, I prayed for a horse to be there when I woke up, and every morning, I opened my eyes with hope, only to feel the familiar pang of disappointment.

But God has a sense of humor, and He never forgets the seeds He plants in our hearts.

Life went on. I grew up. My life centered around school, career, and motherhood. The closest I came to a horse was glimpsing one in a field. But when I was forty-two, I received a gift certificate for riding lessons. From the very first moment I settled in the saddle, I was hooked. I was at the barn every chance I got, and when I wasn't there, I was online researching anything and everything horse. I wanted to learn it all.

At the same time, my children were getting older and more independent, and I began to feel an aching emptiness, a lack of purpose. One evening, while on a walk, I had my headphones on when the words of a song pierced my heart: "God, break my heart for what breaks Yours." Without hesitation, I whispered, "Yes! Do that in me. Use me to make a difference in this world."

I had no idea how literally that prayer would be answered.

A few months later, I stumbled upon a website for a local horse rescue. Until that moment, I didn't know horse rescues even existed. On the screen was an image that broke me: a skeletal horse, lying down because she was too weak to stand. At the auction, they had beaten her so she would walk across the floor, only for her to be sold for a few hundred dollars, loaded onto a trailer, and shipped to slaughter.

I couldn't eat, I couldn't sleep, and when I tried to explain my grief to a friend, I said through tears, "I'm in physical pain. It feels like my heart is broken." In that moment, I knew my purpose: I was called to rescue horses.

I couldn't ignore the pull. Yet, on paper, it made no sense. I was just a suburban mom who had only recently taken up riding. I had no land, no money, no connections. I told everyone I met – neighbors, friends, waiters, strangers – that I was going to start a horse rescue. I figured if I said it enough, eventually I'd tell the right person.

And one day, I did. A woman who was building an equestrian center listened and said, "Okay. I have the land. Let's do it." Together, we began the long process of creating a nonprofit organization. Around the same time, a friend told me about a young horse in danger of going to auction. "Just come look," she said. Against my better judgment, I went and when that skinny horse followed me around the paddock, I knew he was mine. His name was Teddy.

Teddy was playful, puppy-like, endlessly curious. He stole my phone out of my pocket, played with sticks and balls, and trotted over to greet me every time I arrived. He set the standard for the kinds of horses I wanted to rescue: young, overlooked, full of potential. I thought, *Yes, this I can do.* I wouldn't rescue the old, the sick, the starved, and the injured. There was no way I was going to an auction to see those traumatizing situations and conditions. I would rescue horses like Teddy who had fallen through the cracks and just needed some TLC and a little training and then I would find them a good home. That was the plan.

I dubbed the rescue, Nalani (which means The Heavens). We got our nonprofit status in the spring and held our first fundraiser in the fall. And by that time, we had even found a good adopter for Teddy. And even though the thought of him leaving killed me, I knew that I had to let him go in order to save another horse. So, I started to think about where we would find our next horse. We were on our way.

But God had other plans.

One crisp fall day, I went riding with my trainer. As we were giggling and joking, my eye caught a black plastic bag on the ground, and a jolt of fear shot through me. You know those moments that come in a flash where you can see impending disaster and you're powerless to stop it? I knew this wasn't going to be good. The wind caught the plastic bag and sent it billowing into the air. In the blink of an eye, the training pony I was riding spooked, launched himself sideways and bolted, flinging me out of the saddle. I crashed hard on the sand of the riding ring and landed on my left side in a twisted heap. *It's okay, I'm okay,* I thought. And then I saw the hooves of my trainer's horse charging towards me. There was no time to get out of the way. Everything slowed as I stared at the hooves closing in on me in a cloud of sand. A sharp kick near my right shoulder sent me onto my back. I lay splayed on the ground as the hooves pounded-me.

With a sickening *crunch,* a front hoof landed in the middle of my chest. *Umpf.* All the air left my lungs. I grimaced as pain ripped through me. And then a back hoof kicked my left ribs, turning me onto my side. *Now I'm not ok.* Time stopped as I lay there in shock and disbelief, trying to grasp the severity of my situation. Replaying the horrifying scene in my head, over and over. Morbid thoughts crashed through my mind. *You don't survive something like this. I'm not going to survive.*

I waited thirty minutes for the EMTs' ambulance to arrive and when they saw the extent of my damage, they summoned a helicopter to transport me to Fairfax Trauma Center. As they were rushing me in one machine and then another for scans, all I could think about was getting back to the barn to take care of Teddy. It wasn't until I overheard the doctors say, "We need to chest tube her" that the stark reality of my condition settled in. One hot tear rolled down my cheek. I mean, we've all seen Grey's Anatomy. No one wants a chest tube, right?

I survived, but just barely. The doctors told me it was a miracle. They also told me to give up horses. And to add insult to injury, a few days into my hospital stay, I learned that Teddy's adoption had fallen through. But twenty-four hours after I was discharged, I led Teddy back to his paddock. Four months later, wearing a safety vest, I climbed up the mounting block onto his back and Teddy carried me calmly, as though he knew how fragile I was. In that moment, I realized: I hadn't just rescued him. He had rescued me.

That experience shifted everything. I no longer wanted to play it safe. I went to the auction – the very place I had once sworn to avoid – and I rescued a horse who was old, starved, and broken.

Over time, Nalani Horse Rescue grew and, to date, we've saved over forty horses. Some we've rehabilitated and rehomed. Others, like the horse so frail she could not walk across the auction floor, we saved only so they could be spared the final cruelty of slaughter.

In many ways, I have come full circle – from the photo that first broke my heart to the moment I realized that even saving one horse matters.

I carry the understanding that this journey has given me into every part of my life. Three points that guide my steps:

1. Remember your childhood dreams. God often plants purpose in us early, in the form of joy. For me, it was horses. But the horses were only the doorway. What God really gave me was a platform to connect with people, to share His light and His love.

2. Pay attention to what breaks your heart. That's often where your calling lies. We may not be able to solve the world's problems, but we can make a difference for someone – or something. And that matters.

3. Don't limit yourself. When I prayed for a horse in my backyard, I thought that would be enough. But God's vision was so much bigger. Step by step, He equipped me for a mission I could never have imagined.

As I reflect on this journey, I can't help but think of Elaine LaLanne. Like me, she took something she loved – movement, vitality, health – and allowed it to become a lifelong purpose. She didn't keep it to herself. She turned it outward, inspiring countless others to live longer, healthier, more joyful lives. And just as my journey with horses became a platform for healing – for both horses and people – Elaine's journey became a platform for wellness and resilience.

The first time I heard Elaine talk about her life, she shared that perseverance has been a constant thread woven throughout her story. That resonated deeply with me. Because purpose rarely unfolds without resistance. It requires staying the course when the road is long, the work is hard, and the outcome is uncertain. Just as my journey with horses has demanded endurance – physically, emotionally, spiritually – Elaine's journey called her to keep showing up, again and again, for the good of others.

She also said something else that stayed with me: everything she has done has come from her heart. Not strategy. Not recognition. Heart. And in that, I saw myself. I didn't have the experience needed to start a horse rescue; it was about responding to what moved me at the deepest level. By following what stirred our hearts and persevering through the seasons that tested us, our passions became platforms – hers for wellness and resilience, mine for healing, for both horses and people. Living with purpose, I've learned, means living in service – to others, to God, and to the world around us.

Elaine's legacy is a reminder that purpose doesn't retire. It endures. It grows. It multiplies. When it is rooted in the heart and sustained by perseverance, it becomes something far greater than a single lifetime.

Cherry Tapley

Cherry Tapley is the founder and Executive Director of Nalani Horse Rescue in Virginia. A lifelong horse lover, she discovered her true calling later in life – rescuing and restoring horses who had been forgotten or cast aside. Through their healing, she found her own, a journey she shares in her memoir *The Crushing Season*. It's a story of faith, heartbreak, and redemption that reveals how even in our most broken seasons, purpose can be born. Today, Cherry also leads Nalani Encounters, helping people find peace and growth through the wisdom of horses.

Website: https://www.nalanihr.org/

Connect with Cherry:

FB: Cherry Tapley

IG: @cherrytapley

Chapter 20

From a Dream on Paper to Finding Myself

By Deirdre Barnes

As a little girl, I often played "office." Using an old telephone, a manual typewriter, and the Sears catalog, I pretended to take orders over the phone and type them out. I had no idea then how much that play would foreshadow the life I would one day create.

I also grew up watching Jack and Elaine LaLanne on television with my mother and grandmother. Moving along with their exercises and seeing their strength, I also noticed the kindness and joy they radiated. They planted seeds in me that stayed quietly tucked away for many years.

Decades later, while working with Scriptor Publishing Group, I had a front row seat as Greg Justice spent time with Elaine while writing *Pride & Discipline: The Legacy of Jack LaLanne*. Watching her joy and energy at that stage of her life made an impression on me. Her zest for living was contagious. When I look back on my own life and the path I walked to create my Virtual Assistant business, I see that same spark in myself. My wish for every woman who reads this is that you see that spark in yourself, too. Never hold yourself back for the comfort of others. Believe in your dreams and let your light shine from within.

In 1996, I wrote down a dream on a simple piece of paper. I wanted to work from home. I wanted to be present for my family and still build a career. At the time, I had no idea what that business would be, but I believed it was possible. I had watched my father, Charles Barnes, support our family as an entrepreneur through painting, wallpapering, and other businesses. I saw my mother, Deloris Barnes, travel and teach quilting with great success. I knew it could be done.

Back then, Virtual Assistance was not a well-known industry. The internet was still new and there was very little information available. God placed me exactly where I needed to be so that I could begin preparing. While working as a secretary in a training department for state social workers, I had access to every Microsoft Office course from beginner to advanced. I took every class offered, and the one that made the deepest impact was Access, where I learned how databases worked.

I loved using those new skills. I was even asked to teach a group of women who were transitioning off state assistance. Helping them learn and watching their confidence grow gave me joy and showed me how much I loved teaching others. I volunteered to fix a database for special needs children that had stopped working. It was rewarding to find the issues and watch things function again. Those experiences gave the confidence to create the career I have today.

Soon, friends started asking for help. One needed updates on websites built long before the days of WordPress. Another needed help with medical transcription. I loved the work. I was actually doing it!

Then, in 2005, I found VANA (VAnetworking.com), run by Tawnya Sutherland. I discovered that what I wanted to do had a name: Virtual Assistance. I devoured every article, listened to every podcast, and learned everything she shared. I felt an urgency that I did not fully understand at the time, but later I realized it was God preparing me for what was ahead. My marriage was falling apart, I had three young children, and I needed this business to support us.

In 2006, I officially launched Deirdre's Virtual Office. At first, I sub-contracted with other VAs and continued building my skills and taking training courses. Then in 2010, Ashley Mahaffey found me on Twitter and reached out. That connection introduced me to fitness professionals who then became clients. I helped them with their marketing and websites, and many of those relationships continue today.

During those early years, my home life was heavy with loss and hardship. My mother passed away in 2004, and my marriage ended soon after. Those years tested me in ways I had never expected. Through it all, my VA business became my anchor. It allowed me to take care of my children, attend their events, drive them where they needed to go, and still have a career that brought me joy.

Yet even while building something valuable, I carried doubt. I hid behind my business name, afraid to be the face of it. I often questioned whether I was good enough. I struggled with imposter syndrome, and at times, I even sabotaged myself. I pushed opportunities away because I did not feel worthy of them.

A turning point came in 2022 when my daughter asked why I spoke so harshly to myself. I had never considered how it sounded to her. Her words made me stop in my tracks. I realized I did not need to keep tearing myself down. Slowly, I began practicing self-love. I stood in front of the mirror and said, "I love you." At first it felt strange, but then I smiled. I started celebrating small wins, praising myself for doing the laundry or for serving a client well. I started believing myself.

From there, change began to ripple through my life. I started caring for my body with yoga, better food choices, and kayaking. My blood pressure dropped to a safe level, and I released weight. I became friendlier, and my relationships with my children, now young adults became so much more loving. I hired a life coach to help me move through lingering issues. My confidence grew, and so did my business.

This year marks my twentieth official anniversary as a Virtual Assistant. What started as Deirdre's Virtual Office has grown into Atypical Business LLC, with team members and long-term clients who have trusted me for many years. Through the ups and downs, the constant has been my love for this work. I can hardly believe it has been two decades.

Over the years, many women have asked me to sit down with them and explain what I do. I have seen them take those conversations and build incredible careers of their own. Heather went from being a stay-at-home mom to building a thriving business in social media management. Tracy, a homeschooling mom, grew a career supporting well-established companies. Jessica Rowan, my daughter, left a fast-food job and created a successful Virtual Assistant business. Watching them succeed confirmed something inside me. My story was not only about my own success. It was also about creating a path for others.

I realized that all the knowledge I had was waiting to be shared. I felt a deep calling to teach other women how to take control of their lives. That is why I created my Virtual Assistant course. I wanted to give women more than encouragement. I wanted to give them the tools to build careers they could carry anywhere.

Each of the women mentioned above started their journey with uncertainty, unsure if they could really make this work. They questioned their skills, their confidence, and whether anyone would take a chance on them. Yet with every step forward they built something that not only changed their circumstances but also transformed how they saw themselves. Watching their success has been one of the greatest joys of my own career. It strengthens my commitment to keep coaching, because

I know that every woman who learns these skills carries the power to create a ripple effect that reaches far beyond her own life.

Inside the course, I teach the practical side of being a VA – how to set up services, create packages, manage clients, market effectively, and use technology to support business owners. But even more important than skills, I teach the mindset shifts that create confidence. Software skills open doors, but self-belief keeps those doors open.

When I sit down to write a new course module, I see five women:

1. The woman living paycheck to paycheck, unsure how she will make it to the end of the month.

2. The woman in a marriage where she feels trapped, afraid she cannot survive on her own.

3. The young mom who loves being a mother and wife yet longs to find herself again, knowing she has more to give.

4. The woman who is weary of the daily grind of working for someone else and dreams of freedom.

5. The woman who is not ready to retire but is ready for something new and more fulfilling.

I see their strength even when they cannot see it for themselves, and I want them to know what I discovered. *If I can do it, so can you.*

Through the years, I have learned to listen to my intuition, what one of my clients, the author and coach, Martha Beck, calls the Body Compass. I discovered that success can be welcomed with ease. I came to trust myself more fully and began caring for my spirit as much as my work. In the process, I uncovered something far more valuable than a business.

I found me.

Deirdre Barnes

Deirdre Barnes is the founder of Atypical Business LLC and a Virtual Assistant coach. For over twenty years, she has worked as a VA with clients around the world while also raising her family and proving that a business from home can be both sustainable and rewarding.

As other women noticed her success, they began asking how they could do the same thing. Deirdre started mentoring these women through one-on-one conversations, sharing what she had learned and encouraging them. Over time, she saw the same questions asked over and over. That's what led her to create the Virtual Assistant Mastery course.

Deirdre's teaching reflects her belief that success is not built only on software and services, but also on courage and self-love. She guides women to see the skills and strengths they already have and to take steps toward the life they want. Her greatest honor is watching her students build businesses that change their lives and the lives of their families.

As she marks her twentieth year in business in 2026, Deirdre continues to serve clients and mentor women. She believes every woman deserves the chance to create a legacy that lasts. If something in her story has stirred a spark in you, she invites you to explore her Virtual Assistant Mastery course and see if it might be the right path for you, or perhaps for someone you love who is looking for a new direction.

Today, Deirdre and her daughter Jessica Rowan, who also runs a successful VA business, share a home in Kentucky on a hobby farm with their pets.

You can connect with her and schedule a call at www.OnlineCareer-Mastery.com and follow her online:

Facebook: https://www.facebook.com/atypicalbusinessllc

Chapter 21

Finding Your Voice

By Lisa Gleason - *formerly known as Lisa Berman*

To & From a Woman on a Mission

For decades, I've had the privilege of coaching individuals through transformation. As a Mind, Body, and Life Coach, speaker, writer, and healer, my work lives at the intersection of wellness, leadership, and growth. I guide clients through development not just in how they move or perform, but in how they see themselves. The women I choose to work with are committed to living their personal best life for the purpose of making a powerfully positive difference — physically, emotionally, spiritually, personally, professionally, financially, locally and globally. My mission is simple and profound: to help people, especially women, remember who they are, why they are here, to trust their inner voice, and live with gratitude, joy, courage, vitality, and purpose.

Defining Moments

My love of fitness started as a skinny little girl... roller skating scabbed knees, ballet was my love, and my very favorite was the moment my dad got home from work. I could hardly wait to go to his "Garage Gym" where he taught me to "lift heavy", with "excellent form" and to "stay strong". He taught me to stretch properly and even rigged rope pulleys from the garage beams that prepared me for decades later to *get* Pilates & TRX when I first saw it. It was like a whole body of work & set of tools that planted my roots. He taught me self-defense, punching, kicking and introduced me to meridians & areas of endangerment, proper form, concentration, spotting techniques... He benched and deadlifted what I remember to be *a ton* but could straddle split a wall & do a pretty solid round house kick. He taught me mind & body balanced training and even had motivational quotes all over the walls preparing me for my future as a mindset coach.

I began as a socially shy but curious and people-loving girl and an early orthopedic patient undergoing four major reconstructive knee surgeries prior to age 15. With physical education being compulsory in middle school, I was in special ed PE because I couldn't be bumped on the field or switch directions quickly as many sports require without dislocating my knees. Like my heroes, I wanted to be an orthopedic surgeon and a Super-Mom. My surgeons and therapists ultimately led me to be physically solid and gym ready; my mom was always by my side with her work and crochet in tow for the endless hours she would sit by my hospital bedside, therapy and doctors' waiting rooms. In high school, I geeked on science while my parents set aside resources for med school... A gym job seemed like a perfect place for a kinesiology student. Enter one of my greatest life pivots... Family Fitness Centers, (later to become 24 Hour Fitness), on Katella Blvd. in Los Alamitos... It was home of the Life Cycle created by Ray Wilson... and to the people and opportunities that would feed my passion, curiosity and a deep desire to feel fully alive in my own body and life.

My first gym boss fed my passion for growth physically, mentally, spiritually, personally, and professionally. My earliest assignments were to digest Og Mandino's, *The Greatest Salesman in the World*—a story and guide to the true spirit of service—to check in daily with Chris at the nutrition center, and to continue learning through regular books and growth assignments.

It was at this gym that I met who would become my first business partner – a *real* personal trainer, which back then was a rare thing. I never left the gym, making surgery prevention, pre and post op, and holistic empowerment my passion.

I became a trainer, coach, healer, bodyworker, and young entrepreneur signing my first corporate lease at age 20. I worked with many women, spent years practicing listening inward while striving to meet expectations, achieve goals, and "do it right". I learned that it's never *all* "right"! It's an ongoing dance. To make it a masterpiece you must be where your feet are, feel the rhythm, pay attention, stay in touch with your breath, your inner truth, knowing and divine callings.

My earliest defining moments came through initial struggle with and eventually total emersion in fitness and movement of the mind, body and soul. What started as physical training quickly became a mirror—revealing where I was strong, where I held fear, and how to connect with my own deep intuition. Movement, touch, and breath taught me that the body never lies. It stores our stories, our resilience, and our unspoken truths. That journey and discovery drew me in to deep listening, to feeling and hearing the elements of mine and my clients' tissues as a "read" of their ease or *dis*-ease, attunement or misalignment as a major source of knowledge and solutions… if only we can get quiet, tune out the noise and find our own pulse.

Milestones followed through thousands of private coaching and bodywork sessions, owning and operating brick and mortar studios, leading wellness communities, speaking and teaching to groups, and mentoring women navigating both success and burnout. But the most meaningful milestones weren't external.

While highlight reels are so super attractive, adversity has been the most powerful teacher. I've faced seasons of reinvention, personal loss, professional uncertainty, and the humbling realization that growth often requires letting go of identities that once felt safe. There were pivotal decisions where I chose alignment over approval, depth over speed, and purpose over pressure. Each decision refined my voice—less about proving, more about serving which cannot be forced or faked.

Through every chapter, one truth remained constant: when a woman learns to listen to herself, everything changes. Her health improves. Her relationships deepen. Her leadership expands. And her voice—clear, grounded, and authentic—becomes a force for good.

My Connection to Elaine LaLanne's Legacy

Elaine LaLanne represents a rare kind of energy—one that is both powerful and joyful, disciplined and playful. I first met Elaine at Idea World in 2017 when my coach and friend, Todd Durkin was honored with the Jack LaLanne Legacy Award, and from the moment she entered the room at 90 years young and pumped out some pushups on stage with TD, her presence was unmistakable. Her positivity wasn't performative; it was lived, honest, aligned, strong, pure. Her can-do spirit is contagious in the best way!

I'm not a "fangirl" by nature, but Elaine captured my heart. There was something deeply authentic about her enthusiasm, vitality, perseverance, integrity, loyalty to the LaLanne Legacy and her unwavering belief in possibility. She doesn't just talk about strength—she embodies it. She makes wellness feel accessible, exciting, and deeply human.

Elaine's legacy reminds us that fitness isn't about perfection or aestheticism but about life force. It's about showing up fully, choosing joy, and believing that it's never too late to be strong. Her example reinforces that empowerment begins with belief, fueled by consistent, loving action.

Elaine doesn't just inspire movement; she inspires mindset. She's shown me a one-of-a-kind example of how a woman's voice—grounded in purpose and optimism—can uplift generations. Being part of *Her Legacy* feels like standing in that light and carrying it forward with total reverence and gratitude.

Coach Lisa's Offering on Finding Your Voice

Finding your voice is not about volume—it's about truth. It's quiet confidence that comes from knowing yourself and honoring what matters most. Your voice lives in your body, your breath, your choices, and your boundaries. It grows stronger every time you listen to and choose it.

Your inner voice is not loud. It doesn't compete with calendars, notifications, expectations, or urgency. It speaks in stillness. It speaks in pauses. It speaks when you slow down long enough to listen.

Finding your voice requires intention. It requires practices that create space: quiet mornings, reflective walks, journaling, prayer, breath, movement without performance, and moments of solitude without guilt. These are not luxuries; they are leadership practices. They are how you hear your own wisdom beneath the noise.

I believe personal and professional growth is a daily and momentary practice. It's built through small, consistent acts of self-respect: moving and caring for your body with intention, nourishing yourself on all levels without guilt, speaking honestly, resting without apology, and choosing people and environments that support your growth. Empowerment isn't something you can buy, it's something you must tap into and allow to radiate.

For women especially, finding your voice often means unlearning. Unlearning the belief that being strong makes you too much. Unlearning the idea that care for yourself is selfish. Unlearning the habit of shrinking so others feel comfortable. Your voice doesn't need to be justified. It needs to be tapped into and trusted.

Elaine LaLanne shows us that vitality is a choice and joy is a discipline. I invite you to make the same choice—to live boldly, move often, laugh freely, and lead with heart. Your voice matters not because it's loud, but because it is one of a kind, it is yours and "… born for such a time as this". ~ Esther 4:14

When you find your voice, you give others permission to find theirs. You become a living example of what's possible at any age, any stage, and any season of life. And that—more than any title, accolade, or achievement—is the legacy that truly lasts.

Legacy

I hope to leave a legacy not defined by accomplishments alone, but by the lives I've touched and the impact I've made on the people around me. True legacy is relational. It's how we show up, how deeply we listen and the love we give in the moments that matter most.

This is why being attuned to your inner voice is so important. When you live from alignment rather than distraction, your presence becomes a gift. Your choices ripple outward in ways you may never fully see—but they are felt.

If my work has any lasting impact, I hope it reminds women that when you honor your inner voice, you don't just transform your own life—you elevate the lives you touch. That is legacy.

Lisa Gleason

Lisa Gleason, *formerly Lisa Berman,* is a globally recognized Mind, Body, and Life Coach, speaker, writer, and thought leader with decades of experience in fitness, wellness, and personal development. She has conducted tens of thousands of private coaching and bodywork sessions, guiding individuals—especially women—toward sustainable health, confidence, and empowered living.

As the founder of Personal Best Living, Lisa works with mission-driven women, leaders, and entrepreneurs to cultivate strength, clarity, and balance across all areas of life. Known for her warm authenticity and holistic approach, she integrates movement, mindset, and meaningful action to help clients find their voice and live with purpose.

Lisa can be found at **PersonalBestLiving.com** and on social media IG @lisa.berman, FB Linkedin where she shares inspiration, wisdom, and practical tools for living your personal best life.

Chapter 22

Braving the Journey

By Vicki Cable

My life has been filled with adventure and joy. As a child, I once tried out to be a Mouseketeer but instead became an "Imagineer" of my own life. My parents encouraged every dream I had, and because of them, no star ever felt out of reach. Their belief planted the seeds of confidence and curiosity that would shape my journey.

I chose teaching as my profession and never looked back. Teaching gave me the privilege of sharing subjects I loved, coaching sports, and impacting thousands of students. Summers became seasons of exploration by climbing the "Four Sisters" of the Pacific Northwest: Mt. Adams, Mt. Baker, Mt. St. Helens and Mt. Rainier, as well as bicycling across the country from Seattle, Washington to Minneapolis, Minnesota. Life was rich, active, and full of momentum.

In 2004, while living in Homer, a small village in upstate New York, I received my first cancer diagnosis. The words felt unreal, as if they belonged to someone else's story. Yet even in that moment, I was surrounded by the love from family, friends, students, and an entire school community who carried me through the unknown. I never asked God, "Why me?" Instead, I asked, "How could this possibly be used for good?"

During treatment, there was a moment that quietly shifted everything. I was sitting in a chemotherapy chair, watching the slow drip of medication making its way into my body. Around me were others; some sleeping, some silent, some holding tightly to loved ones. A nurse came by, adjusted my IV, and asked gently how I was doing. I paused, and then I said, "I'm okay." For the first time, I truly meant it. It was then that I realized something profound: life itself was the gift. Not my accomplishments, my titles, nor future plans. The gift was breath, presence, and the ability to love and be loved in that very moment. I did not know what tomorrow would bring, but I knew that this moment mattered. Cancer did not strip life of meaning, it sharpened it. Treatment was difficult, but it gave me time to reflect and reevaluate. I began to ask not only what I was doing with my life, but why. In 2009, those questions led me to teaching in New York City at The Academy for Social Action in West Harlem, where I found deep fulfillment in helping students recognize that their potential was far greater than they imagined. Two years later, as an administrator in Washington, D.C., I experienced the same joy helping educators see their strengths and grow into their calling.

Eventually, I returned home to Washington State, believing that perhaps my teaching chapter had come to an end and that my days would now be spent on the golf course. But once again, life had other plans. I accepted what was meant to be a part-time role at South Whidbey High School. That role became five more years of full-time teaching. It was during that season that I truly learned what impact meant. It was not about accolades or outcomes, but presence, connection, and consistency.

2020 brought my second cancer diagnosis. A different cancer. A familiar shock. This time, though, I was mentally prepared. Surgery was successful, and my determination was unwavering. I understood now that while we cannot control every circumstance, we do have agency. We get to choose how we respond.

Our brains will do what we tell them. If we believe setbacks define us or that struggle means failure, we will stop moving forward. My mindset is recognizing that we have the power to change direction. Every day is not easy, but champions keep going. Even in the hardest days, they know that small steps matter and that today counts.

Out of this season emerged a new calling. I became certified as an IMPACT life coach through Todd Durkin Enterprises and a certified cancer coach through The Cancer Journey Institute. I wanted to walk alongside others facing storms, helping them see that their diagnosis, loss, or hardship did not diminish their worth or limit their future and reclaim strength, purpose and passion. In that same spirit I founded Hopeful Horizons Cancer Coaching and that same desire led me to write "Braving the Journey: Rising Above Life's Challenges." It is a collection of short essays and stories to bring encouragement, foster resilience and bring hope for anyone walking through any challenging storm that life may bring.

Today the golf course is still part of my life but only a part. Why do I play golf?

- Golf challenges me constantly and reminds me of the importance of staying present, of being fully immersed in the moment.

- Golf demands perseverance.

- Urges me to push through challenges.

- Reminds me to never give up, even when faced with obstacles.

- Missed shots are inevitable, but they remind me not to dwell on the past, but to focus on the next opportunity.

My story is one of resilience, of faith and discovering that joy and hope are not found in avoiding storms, but in facing them with courage. What I know now is this: life is not measured by certainty, comfort, or control. It is measured by presence, courage, and love. Every storm taught me this: I am still here, and that alone is a miracle worth living for.

Vicki Cable

Vicki is a former high school Mathematics teacher and administrator and is now located in Lawrence, Kansas. She is the owner and lead coach of Hopeful Horizons Cancer Coaching, which provides coaching to those in or out of treatment, family members and caregivers, navigating their way back to a life of purpose and passion. As a two-time cancer survivor herself, she understands the challenging journey.

Vicki received her professional life coaching training through Todd Durkin Enterprises and The Cancer Journey Institute. She incorporates science backed behavioral and fitness strategies in a supportive and inclusive environment to help those dealing with hardships maintain a sense of purpose and motivation.

Follow Vicki:

Website: www.hhcancercoaching.com
FB: @VickiCable
IG: @Vic_Cable

Chapter 23

Finding Joy in My Struggle to Find Health and Meaning

By Julie Boden Schmidt

Personal Introduction

Every morning, I look in the mirror and see someone I almost don't recognize! How did I become the person reflected in the mirror with a twinkle in my eyes and a smile on my face. How did I reach a point where my personal trainer told me I could afford to gain a few pounds – words I had never heard in my lifetime. How did I become the person I am now?

Let me start from the beginning. I began my journeys early in my life – one for a sense of purpose and the other for health. I didn't want just a 9 to 5 job; I wanted a career that would bring me a sense of accomplishment and joy. I wanted to look as good as I professionally felt. The words used to describe me related to those journeys capture the challenges, successes, and failures: in my first fifteen years – a bit scatter-brained, a daydreamer. Later – organized, problem-solver, visionary and synthesizer. With the exception of scatter-brained, I used all of those qualities as I became more skilled and confident in my professional life.

My search for physical health, however, was not a straight line of success. The stages could be described as a series from toddler through mid-adult years: chubby, plump, chunky, overweight, a "weight problem," and finally, obese. There were moments of success but far too often, they were followed quickly by the return to old patterns of behavior.

In the past, I tended to avoid those moments in front of the mirror, a quick reflection in a store window, or trying on clothes in a "fitting room" (the clothes too often not fitting). When I did look, I saw a woman fatigued from 12-hour workdays. I had found my purpose but I was letting my professional drive get in the way of health. The two goals had to merge if I was to be successful.

Defining Moments on My Journey

Some people set goals for one year, five years, and ten years out. That is not how I consciously approached my life: either an opportunity appeared that I was drawn to (my work) or my pain was enough (health) to move me toward help.

Regarding the latter, I tried almost everything. My journey to fitness was yet to be solidified and successful. To some degree, my professional success contributed to my lack of focus on my health by providing many excuses why I was not successful: I don't have time to work out; I am doing great work even though I am overweight.

I tried everything from diet plans to workout fads - Optifast, Nutrisystem, Pilates, Zumba, Jane Fonda, even watching Jack LaLanne with my mother from the couch. Each attempt brought a few lost pounds and a little more resolve.

My professional life took a very different trajectory. I started out as a teacher but volunteered for a family planning clinic, then became certified as a Physician's Assistant in women's health. I thought I had found my calling until one day I saw this very small ad for an Executive Director of a community health center. Although not well prepared for the position, I applied, interviewed and suddenly was hired! The health center, along with over 1000 others, provided health care to those who would not receive it for reasons of poverty, language, culture, and geography if the center did not exist. One of many memories that demonstrated our mission to serve all happened on a cold fall day when the trees looked like a beautiful tapestry. I was visiting one of our more rural health centers when a tractor pulled up to the front door with a flatbed on which sat a big, soiled sofa, occupied by an extremely overweight man. He knew that despite his appearance and level of poverty, he would be welcomed and treated with respect. Those moments captured my heart and soul – I had found my mission! My joy in my work was boundless.

Connection to Elaine LaLanne's Legacy

I was drawn to Elaine's fitness legacy when she said that at the time she met Jack, she lived on a diet of "chocolate doughnuts, candy, soda, frankfurters, and ice cream for years" (possibly with an occasional cigarette). My diet, too, often boiled down to carbs in every shape and form. In 2017 she was inducted into the National Fitness Hall of Fame. That ability to change her life so dramatically instilled in me the belief that with direction and commitment, I, too, could be as successful in my search for health as I was professionally.

Plus, she has spunk! She is not the traditional "old lady," and I don't want to be one either. I want to continue to surprise my children (as she perhaps has surprised the fitness world) with my strength and flexibility – I can still touch my toes with my hands! Elaine is not just young at heart, but young in body – truly my role model.

My Message of Empowerment

I went from over 300 lbs. to 194 lbs., plateaued and then plateaued again at 180 lbs. – all planned, finally. I changed my eating habits, worked out with a personal trainer, and slowly the pounds came off. Then fate intervened: hip replacement followed by infection and a 20 lbs. gain overnight from edema; shoulder replacement, and finally, a diagnosis of advanced cancer. That moment of hearing the diagnosis is permanently etched in my brain and my thoughts were a jumble: Am I going to die soon? What do I need to do to prepare? How can this happen to me? Out of that personal chaos came a strong resolve to fight and continue my journey to health – with an unexpected hiccup. Miraculously, I came out cancer-free and 40 lbs. lighter. For the first time in my life, I understood the mantra of so many weight loss programs: "no food tastes as good as losing weight feels."

The lesson for me was *not* to get sick and lose the weight. It was that being mindful of what I needed to do to be healthy, being positive, having faith in my ability to become healthy and strong, doing the best I could in the moment, having resilience, were keys to becoming and staying healthy and fit. There also were outside motivators (lessons – find them where you can): normal BMI – body mass indicator; wearing a size of clothes that I couldn't remember wearing ever; not worrying about fitting into a regular airline seat or restaurant booth.

Closing Thoughts and Legacy Statement

I want to be remembered as someone who cared deeply - for others and for myself. Like Elaine, I learned that self-care is not selfish; it's how we sustain our ability to give. My legacy is a life lived with purpose, gratitude, and resilience – a reminder that it is never too late to find joy and meaning in both work and health.

Julie Boden Schmidt

Julie Boden Schmidt spent much of her career in healthcare but always dreamed about writing. A great mystery fan, she assumed if she ever pursued that dream, it would be, of course, a mystery. Then, one day while working in remote Montana, she saw three photographs of wood ducklings preparing to leave the nest – by jumping! Her curiosity was roused and imagination stimulated about what it was like to take that jump. That thought was the inspiration that led to her first published children's book, *Woody's Big Leap*.

Julie currently resides in Kansas and continues to use her imagination to inspire those around her as well as her writing.

You can find Julie at www.juliebodenschmidt.com.

Chapter 24

Motion as Medicine, Intuition as the Guide

By Tracy Markley

I've powered through a lot in my life – family loss and heartbreak, hearing loss, learning struggles, danger, divorce, miscarriages, a step-daughter with bone cancer, and serious injuries. Some seasons I pushed forward with strength; in others, I crawled. Through it all, two things kept me moving: I trusted my intuition, and I moved my body. Together, they became my mental health, my protection, and the foundation of my life's work.

Moving my body has always been my anchor. As a child, I wasn't aware it was good health. I just knew, when I was outside doing cart-wheels, handstands, and running around, I always felt joyful, no matter what was happening around me.

I've been in the fitness industry for 30 years. Wow! That sounds like I'm old. I'm turning 60 this year, but I still feel like I'm in my 30s.

In the 1980s, I did a little modeling. I was even on a cover of the Pennysaver for an athletic club ad. When I was 21, I went to meet a photographer who was making a bikini calendar. This was a crazy experience. First, his studio and staff appeared professional and safe. But when I was talking to the photographer, he told me I needed to lose weight. I was 5'7" and 114 pounds. He fixated on shrinking me beyond healthy. I thought at the time, I have no weight to lose. I left our meeting with a gut feeling to avoid this man and not to work with him. It was not because of what he had said to me, it was an inner knowing, a vibe, an intuition telling me don't trust him.

This photographer had called me and told me he wanted me to be one of the models in his calendar. My warning vibe of him was so strong, I came right out and told him, "I have a weird vibe about you. Unless that goes away, I will not work with you." A week later he called me again. I told him the same thing. Then about a month later I got a call from the L.A. police department. They had found my photo and phone number at the photographer's studio. I was asked if I was at least 18 years old, because the photographer had just been arrested for child pornography. Of course, I shared that I was 21 years old but had a bad vibe on the guy. I was glad I stayed away from him.

This is an example for women to always listen to their intuition, even if you don't know the details around a specific gut feeling. Our intuition keeps us protected, as well as guides us to good things. One moment of trusting your intuition today may open an unexpected door years later.

When I was in my 40s, I had what is still the most powerful meeting of a client and a human I have ever experienced. As he approached me walking with his walker, my gut said strongly, "There is a larger purpose in knowing this man, beyond his being a client." And, wow, was that gut feeling right! My whole world changed by knowing this stroke survivor.

When I first saw him in his walker, I thought to myself, "Do I know enough to help him?" I had never trained a stroke survivor at that raw of a stage in their recovery. Then my mind instantly went into positive mode, and I knew I had enough knowledge to work with him. That's when I felt the powerful feeling that working with him had a larger purpose.

I did not know how far I could take him in his stroke recovery. Nor did I know what the larger purpose could possibly be. I just trusted the good vibe and the powerful moment.

All those thoughts and vibes took place in my mind and soul within a few seconds of time. This happened during my first sight of him and the few seconds of us approaching one another from across the room to meet. It was quite a powerful few seconds!

Our journey working together was special, beyond words. He wanted his journey shared to help other survivors. This led to my first book, *The Stroke of an Artist: The Journey of a Fitness Trainer and a Stroke Survivor*. He said if his story only helps one person, that one person is worth it.

Although he has since passed away, his story in the book is still helping stroke survivors, caregivers, and professionals worldwide seven years later. I couldn't be prouder of him and myself.

In the past eight years after writing *The Stroke of an Artist*, I have started stroke support groups. And I have spoken at stroke support groups, medical and fitness events, senior facilities, and different organizations. I was also asked to create a stroke recovery training CEC course for the fitness industry, and as of today, I have published 15 books.

I can't imagine, nor do I want to think of where my life would be if I had ignored my gut feeling about that photographer or listened to the two-second initial thoughts that I didn't know if I could help this stroke survivor in his walker.

This is why body care, brain care, soul care, and mindset matter. They all work together as a team within us, and it is not always easy. I've been through many tough times, often wondering why and how things would get better. At times, I found myself fighting to keep from falling into depression.

Taking care of my body – by eating well, exercising, and staying hydrated – has saved me. I know this because when I care for my mind, body, soul, and brain the best I can, I feel more grounded, think more clearly, and hear intuitive messages, big and small, much more clearly. This has become an essential part of my personal health and fitness care.

Often people think taking care of their body is only about losing weight or being thinner. It is so much more than that. Of course, keeping that extra layer of fat away from your organs and not having extra weight on your joints is much healthier for us. It is an especially important goal and habit in life. But again, it is also so much more than that.

During the last few years, I have experienced an overload of grief and losses. I have lost all three of my parents. My father and stepfather died within a few months of each other. Then I lost my mom in 2023. In the last four and a half years, I have endured more than 20 deaths of family and friends. Two of those losses were my dogs. I was processing losses and changes one after another and the grief for all was blended. It took a toll on me.

My mother had pancreatic cancer, and I was with her through it all. I don't like saying I was her caregiver. That sounds like a job. She was my mother, and I was her daughter. I cared for her and loved her through it all. It was a challenging time, but also a special time.

For years, I have had dozens of women come to me after they had spent months, and sometimes years, caring for a parent in their final times. They felt sickly, had body pains, and/or had gained weight. They were sad and still in a heavy time with their grief journey.

There are multiple diverse types of loss and grief felt while experiencing the parents' illnesses, while they are in hospice, and/or dealing with tough situations, such as dementia lasting days, months, and sometimes years before they die. It takes a hit on the soul and body. Knowing all this and helping so many others through it, I never thought in a million years that I would be affected the same way. In fact, within a couple days of my mom passing away, I got a massage and was determined not to get pain or experience anything like I saw my clients go through. "I'm a professional," I said to myself. "I can stop that from happening to me." Well, I was wrong. In fact, sometimes I wonder if it is because I tried so hard not to let that happen to me that I shut down my body's natural ability to cope properly. I won't ever know. And that's okay.

A couple of weeks after my mom passed, I was dealing with massive, unbearable pain in my spine. My MRI showed all sorts of things wrong. Long story short, I spent months trying to heal. I'm going to correct that and say years. It has been over two years since she passed away, and I am still healing. The physical pain is not as intense. It is still there, although, I'm so much better. The pain was the worst I have ever felt, and I was shut down. When I finally understood that some of the pain was coming from the overload of grief that settled in my body, I began to heal better. There was/is a definite physical injury, but the grief multiplied it.

After seeing dozens of professionals, I went to a pain management doctor, whom my orthopedic doctor had sent me.

The pain management doctor told me that he usually agreed 100% with this orthopedic doctor's procedures that he recommended, but not this time regarding me. He told me that he did not want to do any procedures at this time. He said that I have been living in fight and flight mode and grief for so long that my nerves are shot and making my back pain more than the injury would usually cause.

Several months after the pain management doctor had told me this, I was introduced to an amazing chiropractor, who is also a medium and intuitive. He is the best chiropractor I have ever met. And I have met excellent ones. He helped me at a level that my broken soul needed to heal. Because of my back injury, it hurt to drive my car, so he came to my house. He was expensive, but his work was worth it for my care and well-being. In fact, I could not even hold a four-pound weight in my hand. It hurt my back too much. All I could do for over a year was take walks and do limited stretching. Grief and massive pain are a tough combination to have to heal both at the same time.

This chiropractor was extremely tuned in; it is the best way to put it. He is a medium and a chiropractor. He instantly realized that I was holding my grief in my spine. My pain was emotional, as well as physical. We had several visits together, and I feel that he saved me.

A couple weeks after my mom passed away, I noticed an older woman with her roller walker walking by my house every day. I live on a corner, and many people walk by. I live near the elementary school that I went to in the 1970s. This woman looked like the PE coach named Pat, who worked at the school when I went there. Pat had short light hair when I knew her at the elementary school. When we are little kids, every adult seems old to us. I never thought this woman walking by was Pat, but I knew she must be related to her. She looked just like her. One day I went outside and said Hi to her and I asked if she was Pat's daughter. She said, "No, I'm Pat." I was happily surprised. She is 94 and she walks every day. She only uses the roller walker to keep her safe while outside on her walks. At home, she does not need it. She is so incredibly inspiring! I loved that this was Pat and that she remembered me.

I could not exercise with my injury. Everything made it worse. Even stretching. The only thing I could do was walk. I walked slowly.

Somedays, I was so frustrated I cried with pain. Then I would see my friend Pat walking past my house, and I would think, if she could do it, I could do it. Sometimes, I would walk around the neighborhood with her. She is so cute. She has her own iPhone, and we text one another. We've become friends.

Jack LaLanne said "Your health account, your bank account, they're the same thing. The more you put in, the more you can take out." This is a powerful and true statement. In the case of my back injury, if I had not taken care of my health, as I have throughout my life, it would have been worse. And I would not have healed as far as I have.

We can't always control what trials come into our lives, but we can take the best care of our health. The stronger we are as we enter a battle, the better we come out on the other side.

I published two books in this back pain journey. It was hard to sit too long, so, I sat and then walked, then sat and then walked. It was all I did for a long time. I must be productive or have a creative project going, so, I powered through. I published my second children's book in August of 2024. It is called *Rhyming Riley, The Dog That Rhymes All the Time.* I had adopted a labradoodle from a family around the block whose parents died. The dog needed a home. The story in the book is Riley telling the story of his life with me in rhyme. A special book!

I just published another book a couple weeks ago. This book is called *Balance, Walking, and Fall Prevention – A Fitness Trainer's Guide for Seniors and Pre-Seniors.* I love to share my knowledge to help others and encourage them to take care of themselves.

After my first book, *The Stroke of an Artist,* was published, I began receiving emails, Facebook messages, and phone calls from stroke survivors, personal trainers, and caregivers nationwide asking for more help. That is when I began a stroke support group on Facebook. It grew quickly to more than 5,000 members. Stroke survivors worldwide were desperate for help to get their lives back. I had members from 17 different countries. It was surreal, I was now helping stroke survivors worldwide.

One young man in Maharashtra, India, who had a stroke, sent me a video of him doing exercises. He had asked me if what he was doing would help him and if he had good form. The video saddened me. The equipment was old and rusted, and he was outdoors in the dirt. He also had horrible form. I made him a video to show him exercises and tips to help with his form.

I was contacted by a woman whom her 83-year-old husband had a stroke. She shared stories of trainers and therapists that shocked me. She asked if they could come to the small town I lived in at the time and stay for 30 days so he can train with me every day. They traveled 3,000 miles and did just that. I was honored, but my heart ached for them.

I asked the stroke survivors in this support group what challenges they have had while trying to find good guidance with personal trainers to continue their recovery after their physical therapy has ended. That is for those who were lucky enough to get physical therapy. Many said, "They treat us all the same. They need to understand that not all stroke survivors are the same." They were referring to physical therapists and personal trainers. Several others said, "Personal trainers don't know muscles." They also shared that they were treated like they were irrelevant.

I needed to help all these people the best I could. I had to help educate both survivors and caregivers. This is when I decided to write the book, *Stroke Recovery – What Now? When Physical Therapy Ends, But Your Recovery Continues*. I also began making YouTube videos to help them as well.

When Covid shut us down and survivors could not get their therapy, I personally had an 82-year-old stroke survivor whose hand movements were just beginning to come back when his doctor told him not to leave the house during Covid. It broke my heart.

I then made arm recovery videos and wrote the book, *Stroke Recovery – Regaining Arm Movement*. Then quickly after several survivors asked me if I could write a book on legs and walking. I then wrote *Stroke Recovery – Leg Stability and Walking Gait*. I published two books in three months when my studio was shut down. I felt so bad for those survivors who could not get their therapy. I had to share the knowledge I had. Knowledge is Power!

I am thrilled that I trusted my intuitive vibe of knowing that first stroke client was for a larger purpose. Since then, I have been able to help thousands of stroke survivors worldwide. And that's a very large and important purpose!

When Jack LaLanne said; "Your health account, your bank account, they're the same thing. The more you put in, the more you can take out," I find that it fits for physical, mental, and spiritual well-being.

If we are physically healthy, we can move better, stronger, and for longer. We feel more stable – physically and mentally – and our brains have more clarity. It's easier to be focused and live in the moment. That's when we heal better. That's when we feel more connected to ourselves and better able to recognize intuitive cues.

And that's when we make better choices, especially for our safety and during those small, powerful moments that may lead to larger purposes.

Tracy Markley

Tracy L. Markley is an award-winning personal trainer, educator, and author whose work has become a trusted resource for stroke survivors, families, caregivers, and health professionals worldwide. She is the author of fifteen books, including The Stroke of an Artist: The Journey of a Fitness Trainer and a Stroke Survivor, first published in 2017. Drawing from both professional expertise and lived experience, Tracy bridges the gap between rehabilitation, fitness, and real-life recovery.

With more than 25 years in the fitness and health industry, Tracy is recognized for her leadership in stroke recovery, balance training, functional movement, and fall prevention. Her approach extends beyond exercises, focusing on restoring confidence, independence, and dignity after life-altering medical events. As of December 2025, her books have earned 37 awards, reflecting the depth, credibility, and global reach of her work.

Tracy has been named one of America's Top Fitness Educators by the National Fitness Hall of Fame (2024) and is the recipient of the IDEA World Personal Trainer of the Year Award (2021). Her methods are trusted by fitness professionals and sought out by families searching for safe, effective, and compassionate recovery pathways.

She is the owner of Tracy Markley's Fitness and the creator of the Advanced Education Stroke Recovery Training Course and Functional Anatomy 101 & Beyond, continuing education programs designed to elevate standards in rehabilitation-informed fitness.

When stroke changes a life, Tracy L. Markley's work reminds families that recovery is possible – and that they are not alone.

Connect with Tracy L. Markley

Website & Education Programs: www.tracymarkley.com
Books on Amazon: www.amazon.com/author/tracymarkley
Instagram: www.instagram.com/motivate_healthfit
Podcast: **Host of *The Health and Fitness Show Podcast***
YouTube: www.youtube.com/c/TracyLMarkleyFitnessAuthor

Chapter 25

THE FITNESS FIX

By Janet McLoughlin

From as far back as I can remember it's always been about fitness. It started with sports like T-ball, soccer, and street hockey when my brother would let me play. It was also hiking, field hockey, softball, and basically everything EXCEPT basketball. I'm tall which usually got coaches excited, until they saw my moves on the court. Think of Elaine from Seinfeld's full body dry heave, but with a ball. But finally, my height did pay off in college when I was recruited to the crew team. I never thought I would have so much fun rowing around a dirty river in the dark, freezing to death with my lungs and legs on fire, but it turned out to be one of my happiest places on earth. So, sports were my identity, my passion and a bit of an obsession.

There was nothing worse than showing up to the first day of high school softball practice out of shape. Basketball was out (Elaine!), so I did what any highly motivated, slightly delusional teenager would do. Armed with the latest issue of Muscle & Fitness, some money from my parents (this place was not cheap, thanks Mom and Dad), and a fake ID because you had to be 18 (and no, I did not use it to buy beer), I confidently marched into our local gym.

Up to that point, my only exposure to fitness outside of sports was working out to Bodies in Motion on TV with my "boyfriend in my head," Gilad. I had no clue what I was doing, but I was committed to being fit, strong, and yes, I wanted a six-pack. What surprised me was that the more I went, the less it had to do with how I looked. It became about how I felt. And I felt great.

Great enough that the gym became my refuge. Bad day? Gym. Good day? Gym. Argument with my parents? Gym. Boyfriend broke up with me in the morning, we got back together at lunch, then I broke up with him after school? You know how it was in high school. Gym.

It became, and still is, one of the few places where I feel completely comfortable. It is familiar. It is predictable. Some days I cannot wait to go (hello, leg day) and I leave feeling like Wonder Woman. Other days I drag my ass there, weighed down by stress and anxiety and everything, and somehow a little sweat takes the edge off. It resets my mood, my head, my sanity.

Sadly, at this fake-ID gym, my beautiful refuge, someone struck up a conversation. This was before AirPods, back when people actually spoke to one another. They asked what college I went to. I panicked and blurted out the first one that came to mind, which happened to be the college they attended. Cue internal meltdown, immediate confession, and a rapid, horribly embarrassing exit. I never went back.

I was leaving for college two weeks later, so it was not a total disaster. But wow – was it mortifying.

When I got to college and realized that an engineering degree meant hours hunched over a computer – yuck – I ran for my life. Full sprint out of whatever Engineering Horror 101 lecture hall I was trapped in and straight across campus into the welcoming arms of fitness. I switched majors and earned my degree in Exercise Physiology, and honestly, it felt like coming home.

Once it clicked that my old friend fitness could actually be my career, I went all in. I became an NSCA certified strength coach, a spin instructor, a kettlebell instructor, a TRX instructor. If there was a certification, I probably had it or was working on it. Now I got to share this thing that had carried me for years. I got to show people how movement could support their bodies, reduce injury, steady their mindset, and help them feel better in ways they did not expect – how fitness could fix everything that felt broken and uncertain for them, just like it did for me.

Broken and uncertain showed up again in motherhood. When my son was two and a half, he was diagnosed with autism. Overnight, it felt like I was sitting in the middle of the ocean on one of those flimsy Dollar Store Styrofoam cooler lids, with my son balanced on my lap. Every question felt like a wave hitting us from another direction, knocking pieces off an already questionable flotation device. I was terrified. I was overwhelmed. Thinking about the future felt impossible. The question that haunted me most was simple and unbearable. What happens to him when I am gone?

The gym I worked at had childcare. Thank God. Once again, the gym became my refuge and my anchor. A place where I could step away from the noise and put my hands on a barbell instead of spiraling in my own head. I did not work out to escape my life. I worked out so I could handle it.

That season gave me a new purpose. I stepped into the most meaningful work of my career by working with individuals with autism and creating training approaches that actually worked for them. Needs vary. Abilities vary. There is always a workaround. I've been incredibly privileged to see firsthand how empowering fitness can be for this community – the confidence, the calm, and, as a bonus, a place to belong.

I also saw how badly parents needed support. So, I helped create that space too. A community where parents who are floating on their own Styrofoam cooler of uncertainty can climb onto a big, steady raft with others who truly understand what they're going through – the fear, the questions, and the exhaustion.

I also can't express enough how deeply grateful I am to THE fitness pioneers, Elaine LaLanne (not the one from Seinfeld) and Jack LaLanne. They made movement a movement long before it was trendy. They paved the way to modern fitness as we know it, so people like me could just show up. My life would be very different had they not. I'd probably be hunched over a computer somewhere. And can you imagine no Gilad?

Fitness has been my constant through adolescence, adulthood, motherhood, uncertainty, and growth. It is where I have met some of my closest friends (Yeah BU!), and where I feel most like myself. So yes, I am addicted to working out. Quick disclaimer, like anything, it can be overdone. Please do not overdo it. But this is one habit that gives more than it takes. It builds strength. It brings clarity. It creates connection.

The fitness fix is not about chasing perfection. It is about finding stability, confidence, and a way to show up on the hard days. It reminds us that we are capable of doing difficult things even when we feel unprepared. Does fitness fix everything? No. Will it help? Absolutely.

Janet McLoughlin

Janet is a seasoned personal trainer and coach with over 30 years of experience helping individuals put the pound cake down and achieve lasting results in and out of the weight room. She works with individuals of all ages and abilities and believes in coaching the **whole** person—inside and out.

She holds a Bachelor of Science in Exercise Physiology and a minor in rowing from Boston University and is an NSCA-Certified Personal Trainer and Impact Certified Mindset & Life Coach. Over the years, Janet has accumulated what she jokingly refers to as "about 850,000 fitness certifications," ranging from CrossFit to TRX—partly because they were required (hello CEUs), but mostly because the fitness nerd in her loves learning and bringing new tools to her clients.

The greatest joy in Janet's life is being Ryan's mom. Raising a son with autism has shaped both who she is and how she coaches, inspiring her to create a parent support group and classes designed specifically for individuals with special needs.

To learn more about Janet's work or join her parent support community, visit www.coachjanetmcl.com

Instagram: @coachjanetmcl

Facebook: Janet McLoughlin

Parent Support Facebook Group: It Takes a Village Parent Support Hub

Chapter 26

You Have the Power

By Mary Elizabeth Sadd

It is a pleasure to be part of this body of work with one of the most iconic women of our time! When I think about the fact that it was 1975 before women could have a bank account, a loan and *have* property versus *be* property, it is a reminder of the barriers that Elaine had to overcome many years before her time. She did it all with grace and humility. She created a framework for women who came behind her to model and be empowered. I am particularly inspired by her journey because of my own generational blessings of people who did big things, for the first time that changed history for us and created opportunities that would not be available today without bold moves. My great-great-grandfather was a preacher in the late 1700's in the southeast of what is now the USA. He felt compelled to become an educator so his audience could read the Bible and make a decision for themselves versus being "told" what to believe. He started one of the best academies in the new world and was later recruited to be the president of the University of Georgia. It was the first land grant institution in the US which means the first public, state university. When he arrived in 1819 there were seven students and three administrators. In the 10 years he was there, the University of Georgia grew to several hundred students and became the first version of the UGA we love today. He changed the lives of countless people who would ultimately be impacted by what UGA has become. It's not far off of what Elaine has done for us!

Elaine has not only impacted the fitness industry, but she has had a profound impact on women. She is a pioneer in fitness, she is a motivational speaker and advocate for healthy living…for Pete's sake, we are celebrating her 100th birthday!! She is the poster child of what we need to do and how to live. Her promotion of women prioritizing physical health and well-being, developing a healthy and positive body image is unexpectedly brilliant. She is a trailblazer in the fitness industry! Her enthusiasm, education and dedication to health and wellness have made her a role model for women of all ages. She pulled in nutrition and regular exercise to inform people to make informed choices about health. She is the pioneer of self-care and stress management long before it was popular. Her impact on women has been profound, inspiring them to prioritize health, well-being and personal growth. We all know how women tend to de-prioritize our well-being while we prioritize being in service to others.

My personal journey with health and fitness started in middle school. I was part of the cross country team, mostly out of an interest to be "involved." I found myself at 13 years old to become a pescatarian (that's a fish eating vegetarian). So, no land animals, just seafood, shellfish and fruits, veggies and such. It started when my mother and sister were out of town visiting my aunt, and my dad asked what I wanted for dinner. You see, I was never asked what I wanted for dinner before this time. Ever. Ok, maybe on a birthday here or there but I was raised in a generation where children were to be seen and not heard. You get what you get and don't cause any problems. Over a few weeks when my dad gave me options of what I wanted to eat, I realized I really NEVER wanted to eat meat, but no one ever asked me. I just didn't like it. I loved seafood but we seldom ate it because of my mother's allergies. Dad and

I ate seafood for weeks and weeks…it was fabulous. I may have also been influenced by reading the book "The Jungle," by Upton Sinclair, about the meat packing industry before it was regulated. It grossed me out to think about bloody meat body parts of animals. All that to say, I do not mind if anyone else eats meat and, quite frankly, at 60 years old I struggle to get enough protein without it, but I just don't want it myself.

Back to my journey, I realized the massive impact of what we eat and how our bodies respond. For me, even more than my exercise, my food choices literally shape my body. But the exercise is #2 for me. We have to move, we have to do weight bearing exercise, we have to get our heart rate up, and we need good quality sleep. Moving is the game changer to longevity in my opinion. It's the game changer to keeping bones healthy! As a women with osteoporosis, I have learned that I can't build bone if I don't have estrogen. I can't take estrogen without progesterone while I still have a uterus. My muscles will never out muscle what my bones can handle so I need to build new bone or I don't get more muscle. Nor can I build bone without vitamin D2 and K3. This is not simple but it's important to know how to keep yourself healthy (or get yourself healthy). Seek out options if you are confused or don't know where to start.

If you study Elaine's work, you will see she was an advocate of walking long before it became so popular. It's good to walk every day! If you can move, move more! Everyday…yes, it's that simple.

Some of the qualities of Elaine that I respect massively are her consistency, attitude, humility, healthy eating, physical activity, and purpose. She has always demonstrated a positive mindset and focused on what you *can* do, not what you *can't*. She emphasizes the importance of attitude in aging healthfully. Elaine is incredibly humble, never thinks too highly of herself, and I think she might not really grasp the gravity of her impact on women and healthy living for generations to come! She was one of the first people to draw attention to eating nutrient dense foods to fuel your body, so your exercise gets full impact. She is adamant that physical activity daily is key to your health and youthfulness. She makes a point to find purpose in what you do, not just physically, but also emotionally and having meaningful relationships. It's all part of self-care!

My personal encouragement is to realize you have the power. You have all the power over yourself. No one else, just you. You can start a diet in the middle of a bag of potato chips…it does not have to be Monday or January 1st. Right now is the best time to make better decisions and take decisive actions that prioritize YOU. You are amazing, people need and want you in their lives, so not taking care of ourselves is actually incredibly selfish. Getting a workout and eating "buddy" to check in with can be super helpful. We will often cheat on ourselves but not by others we care about and have made a pact with. And remember, especially if you are a parent, more is caught than taught. I am blessed to have three grown sons that eat amazingly healthy and are lifelong athletes because of what they were exposed to with my husband and I prioritizing work outs and clean eating. We never told them, we just exposed them. Some of my favorite things to do are Pilates, walking, occasionally HIIT class on Peloton. I am somewhat obsessed with Pilates and have been a walker for over 20 years. Peloton is my cardio go-to, and I also have an inversion table I use to keep my back feeling good. I use the ab wheel to keep my core tight. and I recently got a vibration plate that I love. It helps with bone building and overall health. From a nutrition POV, I have a very low metabolism and fortunately a small appetite. So, I have to be very careful to eat the most nutritious food I can or I will be full very quickly on the bad stuff if I don't start with the good stuff. As I mentioned earlier, I am a pescatarian but quite frankly, I love rice and potatoes, so I have a deal with myself. Until I have eaten at least half of my fish and ¾ of my non-starch veggies, I tell myself that I can't touch the rice or potatoes. I am gluten free, but wheat free bread is also part of the off- limits until I have had enough protein and vegetables. Sort out what works for you, think about it....you already know, just do it!

We are profoundly grateful for the legacy of Elaine LaLanne! Have you given thought to the legacy you are leaving? It's not something we can or can't do. We just do it with our daily living. What do you want to be known for, remembered for? What lives are impacted in what ways because of choices you made and courage you have? Have you ever thought about your obituary? What about writing it now and starting to live it now if you are not already? Personally, I want to continue the legacy of learning, earning and returning that I have in my DNA from my great-great-grandfather. I want to out-generous everyone with time, treasure and wisdom. I want to die being in the highest league of givers…not because I have a lot to give monetarily, but because I give generously from what I have. I am reminded of the biblical story of the woman who gave two small copper coins, worth only a few cents, but despite her seemingly small contribution, Jesus said she gave more than anyone because she gave out of her poverty putting in everything she had to live on. (Mark 12:14-44 and Luke 21:1-4)

Mary Elizabeth Sadd

With over 30 years in executive search, Mary Elizabeth Sadd has placed more than 1,000 candidates in their career homes – creating ripples of impact that extend far beyond the workplace. She believes that every placement is more than just a job change; it's a catalyst for transformation in careers, families, and communities.

Mary Elizabeth's passion for people is deeply rooted in her family legacy. Inspired by her Great-Great-Grandfather's philosophy of teaching over preaching, she has dedicated her life to the principle of learning, earning, and returning – a philosophy that defines both her personal and professional journey. She doesn't just help people find jobs; she helps them discover opportunities that elevate their potential and purpose.

A sought-after speaker, Mary Elizabeth brings authenticity, insight, and a passion for service to every stage she steps onto. Whether reflecting on her grandfather's lasting legacy at the University of Georgia or sharing her own journey of impact, she challenges audiences to think beyond success and embrace significance.

Mary Elizabeth Sadd is more than an author and talent connector – she's a legacy builder, a leadership advocate, and a champion of meaningful work.

Chapter 27

5 Winning Secrets I Learned from Elaine
Life lessons from an American Treasure.

By Sarah Sneider

#1. They Can't Keep Us Down!

Hearing a familiar voice, I looked over and was surprised to see Elaine LaLanne walking nearby. She smiled and with a reassuring voice said, "They can't keep us down!" We were at the LA Fit Expo at the Los Angeles Convention Center in 2015. I was there to compete in an AAU Powerlifting event in the bench press and strict curl.

Three-time Emmy winner, Eric Goldfarb, along with Eric Howell, were there filming me for a scene in the documentary *Impossible Dreamers*. An interview with Elaine LaLanne filmed several months later is also included in the movie.

My beloved husband, Harry Sneider, had unexpectedly passed just months before. Elaine's words were so encouraging and unforgettable at the most difficult time in my entire life.

Elaine's husband, Jack LaLanne, had passed four years earlier and her words gave me the courage and determination to keep going on.

Harry was my best friend, soulmate, chief encourager, promoter, always by my side in any competition event, and we had worked side-by-side in a fitness and coaching career for over four decades. Before meeting Harry, I had never been involved in fitness, sports, or competitions. Harry had changed my life for the better.

How does one go on? Elaine was doing it. If she could, I could, too. One day at a time. "They can't keep us down!"

Those five powerful words from the comforting voice of beautiful Elaine LaLanne remain with me today years later. "They can't keep us down!" Thank you, Elaine for the inspiration at the most needed time.

Sarah Sneider, Elaine LaLanne, and Harry Sneider
at IDEA World Fitness Convention in 2011.

#2. Dream Big! Teamwork Makes Dreams Come True!

Harry and I met on a blind date at the Hollywood Palladium! He was a student at Ambassador College in Pasadena California. I had already graduated but was working on campus as secretary to the college treasurer.

Harry invited my co-worker, Kathy Hoyt, to a college dance at the Hollywood Palladium but she already had a date. Kathy suggested he call me. Harry was truly a God-given gift.

I grew up on a farm in rural Missouri and went to a small two-room school, grades 1-4 in one room and grades 5-8 in the other room. Riding a school bus to school every day both in grade school and high school prevented me from participating in extracurricular sports activities after school.

When Harry was 2 ½ years old, he fled Latvia with his mother and 4 year old brother in a cattle car during World War II after the Germans forced his father into military service. While in a displaced persons camp during the war Harry fell, developed osteomyelitis in his hip and faced the real possibility of amputation. Instead, his hip was fused. He had a severe limp and could no longer run or play like other children. Sponsored by a family in Minnesota, the Sneider family came to the U.S. in 1949.

We were married 46 years, enjoyed over 40 years working together in fitness and coaching, have three amazing children, four wonderful grandchildren, and now a great grandchild!

For 23 years Harry was on the Ambassador College Faculty in the Physical Education Department and also Men's Fitness Director. I was Women's Fitness Director at Ambassador for 14 years. We also had many amazing opportunities through The Ambassador International Cultural Foundation. Then in 1990 Ambassador College in Pasadena suddenly closed with very short notice!

We both unexpectedly lost our jobs with only six months' severance pay. We questioned what to do. Where would we go? How would we support our family? It was a very challenging time with two children in high school and one in junior high. After months of deliberation and anxiety, we eventually decided to open Sneiders Family Fitness to continue serving athletes, celebrities, and the community with our knowledge and skills.

I'm so grateful Harry and I were able to work together through the years, travel together, and experience amazing things together. More than I ever dreamed!

Here are some of the highlights:

*Harry and I participated in The Great American Workout on the White House Lawn along with Arnold Schwarznegger, Jack LaLanne, and other fitness pros and athletes including Denise Austin and Muhammad Ali.

*We represented the U.S. at the World Congress on Fitness in Chicago in 1991, where Harry spoke to representatives from 75 nations on fitness and health. He was one of five speakers from the U.S. along with Dr. Kenneth Cooper, the Father of Aerobics, and George Allen, Director of the President's Council on Physical Fitness and Sports.

*At the Goodwill Games in Moscow, founded by Ted Turner to bring nations together through the universal language of sport, we were able to "go behind the scenes" as U.S. coach and official photographer. At the Opening Ceremony, we were seated just yards from Soviet President Mikhail Gorbachev. At the Games we had a wonderful opportunity to meet many Olympic athletes including Peggy Fleming, Bart Conner, Sergey Bubka, and more.

With Harry coaching athletes who were competing, we were at the filming of the American television show Superstars multiple times.

Filmed in the Bahamas, it was a competition of professional athletes including high jumper Dwight Stones, baseball player Steve Garvey, bodybuilder Mike Mentzer, water skier Wayne Grimditch and many others. We had the pleasure of meeting and conversing with Eunice Shriver, mother of Maria Shriver.

Jack and Elaine were an excellent example of teamwork! Teamwork is important for success in nearly every facet of life. By combining diverse skills and strengths we can achieve goals more efficiently and effectively. Whether having a mate, friend, or mastermind group as a support system, teamwork makes dreams come true.

Harry and Sarah Sneider at the Great American Workout
on the White House Lawn in 1992.

#3 If It's to Be, It's Up to Me!

Harry Sneider and I first met Jack LaLanne in 1974, over 50 years ago. Harry had written a letter to Jack about squatting 490 lbs. on one leg since his other leg was fused at the hip. Jack invited us to be guests on The Jack LaLanne Show.

Jack told us, "Anything is possible and YOU can make it happen." Elaine and Jack made it happen. Jack constantly trained, did pushups, and was extremely fit and prepared. He made the call!

While co-hosting a TV show in 1951, Elaine got a call telling her there was a guy who could do pushups through the entire 90 minute show. Elaine made it happen for Jack. She made the decision to say, "Yes!" She agreed to have him do pushups on her show which eventually led to Jack having his own Jack LaLanne Show. Elaine opened the door and Jack walked through it. Elaine put Jack on TV. And as they say, "the rest is history".

I've learned, "If it's to be it's up to me." Ask and you shall receive. When the door is open, walk through it. As Jack and Elaine often said, "Anything is possible and YOU can make it happen!" You can create opportunities. Walt Disney said, "All our dreams can come true, if we have the courage to pursue them."

In 1980, Jack and Elaine invited our family along with Dwight Stones, a world champion high jumper and Olympic medalist training with Harry, to their beautiful home in the Hollywood Hills. Harry and I together developed a total body fitness program called "The Perfect Workout" using a rebounder and handheld soft weights. This was a time when minitrampolines/rebounders were first manufactured and became popular.

Forty-five years later minitrampolines are even more popular due to improvements in design. I'm grateful to have actually jumped with Jack! He endorsed the program Harry and I created and even kindly gave us permission to put photos of him in our *Harry and Sarah Sneider's Olympic Trainer* book. The 40th Anniversary edition of this book is currently available on Amazon. Jack and Elaine truly wanted to help others help themselves.

The Sneider family and Olympic medalist Dwight Stones
visit Jack LaLanne at his home in 1980.

4. Be Kind, Caring, and Have an Attitude of Gratitude

Elaine "LaLa" is the kindest, sweetest person I know. After hearing about my late husband Harry's passing, Elaine wrote a very caring handwritten letter to me filled with encouragement, sympathy and understanding - a letter I will always cherish.

Elaine always makes time for you! Over the years, as a fitness professional, I always looked forward to seeing her at the annual IDEA World Fitness Conventions in LA, Anaheim, San Diego and Las Vegas.

During the 2025 IDEA Fitness Convention in Sacramento, Elaine honored Denise Austin with the prestigious Jack and Elaine LaLanne Lifetime Achievement Award at IDEA World's Golden Gala of Distinction evening celebration. The next day Elaine had multiple interviews for TV, newspapers, and magazines.

At 99 years young she could easily have said, "I'm tired, I think I'll skip this." But she didn't. She showed up that same day at the IDEA Fitness Expo and delivered a wonderful 25-30 minute message while leading a chair exercise session with all of us there. I'll always remember a memorable quote from her message, "Be careful what you put in your mouth". Elaine "La,La" is truly a winner!

Elaine has been my idol and mentor. We have several things in common as well. I also shared a fitness career with my husband. Like Jack, Harry was also an early riser, getting up before dawn. I, too, have a son who loves to surf. Elaine's son, Jon, builds surfboards as well. We both jumped on trampolines, although she's more impressive with splits in midair! I want to encourage others to keep fit and healthy like Elaine. She exudes an attitude of gratitude, positivity, and humor. I deeply admire her speaking ability so very much.

Harry also had some things in common with Elaine. After immigrating to the U.S. at age 8, Harry also grew up in Minneapolis. Like Elaine, Harry went to the University of Minnesota before coming to California. Harry and Elaine also share the same birthday, March 19!

Elaine LaLanne performs splits mid-air on an original minitrampoline.

At the IDEA Fitness Convention in Sacramento, I told her I see her every morning. She looked at me like I was a bit crazy until I explained that her photo is on my refrigerator.

Elaine and I also have a connection with Queen Sirikit of Thailand. When she was president of WAIF, Elaine shared her role in welcoming Queen Sirikit to Los Angeles. As a guest of the Ambassador Foundation, Queen Sirikit also had many activities at Ambassador College including an exhibition at Ambassador Hall beautifully arranged by her staff.

Thailand treasures were on display of gold, silver and gemstone, along with samples of woven silk and exquisite fabrics. The queen was sponsoring the work in Thai villages through her SUPPORT Foundation. With many dignitaries attending, there was a banquet at the Ambassador Auditorium. Queen Sirikit also presented a lecture and documentary at the Ambassador Auditorium to invited guests.

During a tour of the Ambassador College campus, Queen Sirikit visited Harry Sneider in the Men's Weight Room where she observed Harry training athletes with the program we developed using a mini-trampoline and soft hand weights. She was so impressed, Queen Sirikit requested 6 mini-trampolines be shipped to Thailand along with 12 pairs of our soft hand weights for her and her court. Queen Sirikit wanted to stay fit and help her court stay fit!

Queen Sirikit of Thailand at Ambassador College

Queen Sirikit on a tour of Ambassador College
with college President Herbert W. Armstrong.

Elaine makes others feel important. In Vegas she was very busy, but she took the time to come back so I could get a photo with her. While autographing a book for an attendee at an IDEA Fit Expo in LA, she didn't just quickly scribble her initials or name. She very carefully signed the book and also included an encouraging message!

Sarah Sneider and Elaine LaLanne
at IDEA World Fitness Convention in Las Vegas.

My hero and role model, the sweetest, kindest person I know…The First Lady of Fitness! Elaine at 100 continues to be a source of inspiration and encourages us to "Keep on keeping on!"

Elaine LaLanne and Sarah Sneider at IDEA World Fitness Convention in Sacramento in 2025.

#5. You're Never Too Old to Try Something New!

At 98, Elaine set a new Guinness World Record by leading the largest number of people doing Jumping Jacks simultaneously. Seeing Elaine lead thousands of us doing 98 jumping jacks with her at the LA Convention Center during the IDEA Fitness Convention in 2024 was simply amazing.

She continues to host her podcast, make appearances at fitness conferences, inspires through the internet, has interviews for TV, articles in newspapers and magazines, books, and runs BeFit Enterprises and more as she helps the world become healthier and happier!

Bouncing back… After Harry passed, I knew I had to continue working out to stay fit. It's what brought me joy. Bouncing to music on a minitrampoline lifted my mood. I also needed to continue competing in the Senior Games. Senior Games are in every state in the U.S. and for anyone 50 or older. The Games are fun and participants are like family. Never having competed before in high school or college, I began at 50. Now at 81, I'm grateful to continue to compete and will as long as I can.

Sarah Sneider, backed by Harry Sneider, displays medals won at the California State Senior Games where she competed in multiple events in 2011.

You don't stop playing games when you get old. You get old because you stop playing games. Elaine played golf in her 90's. You're never too old to dream big. You're never too old to be a champion.

As Elaine says, we need:

- Something to do.
- Someone to love.
- Something to look forward to.

If you're going through tough times, remember tough times don't last, tough people do. It's not what happens to you, but what you do with what happens to you. It's not whether you get knocked down, it's whether you get up!

What brings you joy? What gifts can you share? What's your story that will inspire others? We grow through adversity. Our pain becomes our purpose. You CAN help others get through their challenges through your example.

May I encourage you to create a life you love living. Believe in yourself. As women, we often put the needs of our husband and children first. Self-care is important. It's like putting your mask on first so you're able to put on the mask of others.

I want to help others achieve excellence, be fit, enjoy life, and reach their fullest potential. I want to continue to carry the torch as Elaine is doing. I'm so very grateful to have Elaine as a mentor and friend. She's a true winner in the game of life!

I want to continue to set a good example to inspire others that they can do it, continue Harry's legacy, and continue the movement to fitness and health that began with Jack and Elaine LaLanne. I want to help make the world healthier and happier.

You are stronger than you think. Dream big! You are a winner! You can do it! Go for it!

Sarah Sneider, 20 years old and 80 years young.

Sarah Sneider

Sarah Sneider, a great-grandmother, is the wife of Harry Sneider, Ph.D., a world renowned authority in fitness education, Olympic coaching, and a world powerlifting champion. She is co-author of their best-selling book, *Harry and Sarah Sneider's Olympic Trainer, 40th Anniversary edition* published in 2021. In 1981, they founded Sneiders Family Fitness, Inc.

Sarah and Harry together developed a simple system involving a mini-trampoline and a set of graduated hand-held soft weights called "The Perfect Workout." They've demonstrated in their own fitness center –with world famous athletes, businessmen and women, housewives, children, retirees, and the disabled –that the system works! They created Sneiders Perfect Rebounding Workout DVD and with son Rob, Sneiders Resistance Rebounding DVD.

The Sneiders have hosted California and Pasadena Senior Games Powerlifting for over 30 years. Starting at age 50, Sarah has also competed in Masters Track and Field and the Huntsman World Senior Games. She now has over 150 medals.

Sarah Sneider, B.A., a fitness professional for over 50 years has been certified by the American Council on Exercise.

Rob Sneider, B.A. Exercise Physiology, M.A. Education.

Along with son, Rob, Sarah continues to train athletes, couples, and anyone wishing to get in the best shape of their life. Sarah credits exercise for helping her get through the unexpected loss of the love of her life, her best friend, soul mate, motivator and encourager – her beloved Harry. They were married over 45 years and have three wonderful children, four amazing grandchildren, and a precious great-granddaughter.

The Sneiders are featured in the film *Impossible Dreamers* by three-time Emmy winner, Eric Goldfarb. As a personal trainer for World Chess Champion Bobby Fischer, Harry's interviews are included in two documentaries Bobby Fischer, *Against the World* and *Bobby Fischer – Anything to Win.*

Photo, hair, and makeup by granddaughter Madison Frausto.

CONNECT WITH SARAH:

Website: www.DrFit.net
Facebook: Sarah Sneider
Instagram: Sneiders Family Fitness
YouTube: Sarah Sneider

Part 3

LaLa-isms

This section gathers the phrases Elaine has lived by. They are simple, direct, and deeply human. Each one reflects how she moves through the world with humor, honesty, and steady self-trust. Some will make you smile. Some may stop you for a moment. All of them reveal the mindset behind a life well lived. Read them slowly. Let them sound like her voice in your ear. These are not quotes to admire from a distance. They are reminders meant to be carried, used, and lived.

- *I don't want to be old when I'm old.*

- *Where I live, I live.*

- *Happiness is me.*

- *There's always a middle ground.*

- *I don't mind talking about my demise.*

- *I don't have a best friend. I can't segregate love like that.*

- *Let's get the thing done.*

- *Everybody's interesting.*

- *Never say never. You'll end up doing it.*

- *I really love people.*

- *I fell in love with Jack's brain, not his body.*

- *Just keep your nose above water.*

- *I face life as it comes.*

- *I don't have any fears.*

- *Learn to love yourself from the inside out.*

- *If you put yourself in other's shoes, nothing can go wrong.*

- *If you don't move, you become immovable.*

- *You have to laugh at yourself.*

- *Some people write the lyrics and some write the tune/music, and then they have a hit song."*

Final Thoughts from Elaine's Friends

My husband Dmitri Bobkov and I met Elaine LaLanne ten years ago. Our friend, Allen Joe, insisted on meeting with Elaine. He said, "You must meet Elaine! She is a great person, just like Jack! And he was right.

Allen met Elaine's husband, Jack LaLanne, in 1936. Allen was a teenager. His father left the family, leaving his mother Florence and his older brother. Allen had never seen his father again. Young man was devastated. His mother came from China and did not speak English. Allen got a job delivering newspapers and bean sprouts, working for Yuen Hop Co, the noodle shop in Chinatown in Oakland. The business is still thriving today. Allen and his wife Annie would take us to buy his favorite vegetables, bitter melon, bean sprouts, and fresh egg noodles.

Allen and Jack met again in Oakland in 1945. World War II is over. Jack opened his first cultural studio in Okland's downtown. He encouraged Allen to train with him. Allen Joe was the first Chinese to win the title of Mr. Northern California at the Multiracial Bodybuilding Competition in at the YMCA in Berkley, California in 1946.

In 1962, Allen met Bruce Lee in Seattle at the Ruby Chow restaurant where young Bruce worked. And they instantly became friends for life, until Bruce Lee's death on July 20, 1973. Everything that Allen learned from Jack LaLanne, he passed on to Bruce Lee who became a legendary martial artist and actor.

When I think about Elaine LaLanne, my heart immediately fills with joy and gratitude for her kindness, friendship, and unwavering presence. Elaine generously shared her time with us, helping us to learn about healthy eating and juicing. We made juice together using Jack LaLanne's juicer from apples, carrots, and celery. It was so much fun!

Elaine is a great storyteller. Dmitri and I can never get enough of the stories about her life with Jack, filled with adventures, travels, running the Jack LaLanne TV Show for 43 years, raising family, inventing products, writing books, and opening the first natural whole food store in Oakland.

Elaine is generous with her wisdom and knowledge, a true pioneer in her own right. She reminded us that having goals and working hard with consistency and patience could help us to reach our own goals and build our own legacy. Elaine is our role model, and her life is a great example of perseverance, compassion, and service. She finds joy and gratitude in ordinary moments- the scent of fresh flowers in her garden, feeding a feral cat named Boots, a company of friends, and she has many friends.

Elaine LaLanne's legacy is simple: to be a true friend, be yourself, and help others who face hardship. Dmitri and I are forever grateful for her unwavering friendship, loving kindness, and heartfelt generosity. She built a beautiful legacy – one that will continue to live on through the compassion and love she shared with us all.

-Svetlana Kim & Dmitri Bobkov

Authors of *The Last Musketeers: Allen Joe's Life and Friendship with Bruce Lee*

About the Author

Elaine is a sparkling, vivacious, motivational public speaker, known and loved by thousands for her warmth, spontaneity, and personal inspiration to others toward a greater joy of living. At 100 her appearances are vital, dynamic and life changing to people of all ages. She stimulates, motivates and educates! Since her early days as a television pioneer, and host in 1948, Elaine has lit up screens all over America.

She was also an integral part of her husband Jack LaLanne's television programs, speaking, and other public engagements. As a solo speaker, Elaine was sponsored by Post Cereal promoting her program and her book, *Dynastride*, a walk and exercise program for all ages. She also toured the country promoting her books. Elaine has invigorated the Jack LaLanne Power and Fusion Juicer infomercials and has made appearances on countless television programs such as The Today Show, The Early Show, Friends, Fox and Friends and Howard Stern. Her unique insight towards nutrition and staying in good physical condition is the reason Elaine was a recurring guest at many places where she spoke.

At 100 she still hasn't slowed down and still does jackknives daily. Her years of experience combined with her contemporary business savvy provide an exclusive insight into Jack LaLanne as she answers everyone's questions about her husband. Her presentations even include footage of some of his superhuman feats of strength! Elaine LaLanne, she looks young, she acts young and inspires her audience to be young at any age! With infectious excitement, she paints a picture of the "YOU" that you want to be.

Follow Elaine at:

https://jacklalanne.com/

And listen to her "Pass it On" Podcast at:

https://jacklalanne.com/youtube

**If you, or someone you know,
is interested in writing a book,
contact us at:**

ScriptorPublishingGroup.com

Listen to our podcast

"It Just Takes One"

at

https://scriptorpublishinggroup.com/podcast/

Follow us on social media:

FB: @ScriptorPublishingGroup
IG: @ScriptorPublishingGroup
Substack: @TheWritersCafe